The Complete Handbook of Science Fair Projects

Related Titles of Interest from John Wiley & Sons, Inc.

Animal Behavior Science Projects, by Nancy Woodard Cain

Plant Biology Science Projects, by David R. Hershey

Janice VanCleave's A+ Projects in Biology, by Janice VanCleave

Janice VanCleave's A+ Projects in Chemistry, by Janice VanCleave

Student Science Opportunities: Your Guide to Over 300 Exciting National Programs, Competitions, Internships, and Scholarships, by Gail L. Grand

The Complete Handbook of Science Fair Projects

REVISED EDITION

Julianne Blair Bochinski

Illustrated by Judy J. Bochinski-DiBiase

John Wiley & Sons, Inc.

New York • Chichester • Brisbane • Toronto • Singapore

This text is printed on acid-free paper.

Copyright © 1996 by John Wiley & Sons, Inc.

The publisher and the author have made every reasonable effort to ensure that the experiments and activities in the book are safe when conducted as instructed but assume no responsibility for any damage caused or sustained while performing the experiments or activities in this book. Parents, guardians, and/or teachers should supervise young readers who undertake the experiments and activities in this book.

Library of Congress Cataloging-in-Publication Data

Bochinski, Julianne Blair, 1966–
    The complete handbook of science fair projects / Julianne Blair Bochinski; illustrations by Judy J. Bochinski-DiBiase—Rev. ed.
        p.   cm.
    Includes index.
    ISBN 0-471-12378-1 (cloth: alk. paper).—ISBN 0-471-12377-3 (paper: alk. paper)
    1. Science projects—Handbooks, manuals, etc.—Juvenile literature. [1. Science projects—Handbooks, manuals, etc.   2. Handbooks, manuals, etc.] I. Title.
    Q182.3.B63 1996
    507.9—dc20   95-22791

Printed in the United States of America

10 9 8 7 6 5 4 3 2 1

To my nephews
Andrew and Alexander

CONTENTS

FOREWORD TO THE REVISED EDITION

Julianne Bochinski has asked me to give my views on the changing direction of science fairs and science fair rules. I was a student participant from 1955 through 1960 in the Connecticut Science Fair and represented Connecticut at the International Science and Engineering Fair (ISEF) in 1958 and 1959. For the past 20 years I have been an active volunteer in the Connecticut Science Fair serving as Chairman of the Board of Directors and, for the past nine years, as Fair Director, providing overall leadership for the fair's yearly and long-range planning. In my day job, I manage electronic systems research at the research center of United Technologies Corporation. My comments come from firsthand experience as Fair Director and from my profession in scientific research, seasoned by science fair memories of my youth. From these experiences and my interactions with Science Service, the organizers of the International Science and Engineering Fair, I have summarized here some of the most important recent changes and trends as I see them.

Science Fair Rules

It is very important that you contact your local science fair as early as possible if you're thinking about doing a science fair project. Rules change from year to year, and the changes usually affect at least some project areas. Contact Science Service, Inc., 1719 N Street, N.W., Washington, D.C. 20036 to obtain an ISEF rule book. The ISEF rule book is essential for understanding the rules governing your choice of topic. Find out from your local fair director about the registration procedure. Important, and sometimes not obvious, differences do occur from fair to fair to adjust to unique operational and community situations. It is important for you to understand how your local fair may differ from what is described here.

The overall direction of science fairs nationwide is set by Science Service, which conducts the ISEF and the Westinghouse Science Talent Search. Each ISEF-affiliated fair is entitled to send two individual student projects and one team project to the ISEF. The ISEF requires each of its charter affiliates to comply with its rules and regulations. Failure to do so can result in loss of its charter and right to participate in the annual ISEF. The ISEF is limited to students in grades 9 through 12 who have not reached age 21 by May 1. Only the work you did since the last ISEF will be considered during judging.

The rules of the ISEF, while straightforward in purpose, have become a challenge for students, advisors, and the fair committee. What has changed in recent years is not so much the rules but the level of enforcement of the rules.

Topics

Certain topics must be approved by a scientific review committee before you begin your research. The ISEF research approval process is intended to ensure student safety and eliminate any unauthorized research at the outset. Approval prior to the start of research is required for any project involving animals, humans, pathogenic agents, or recombinant DNA. Vertebrate animal and recombinant DNA research is not allowed except in institutional/industrial settings. Each fair is required to have a scientific review committee and an institutional review board to review and approve, as appropriate, all projects in the fair. See the ISEF rule book for full details.

Be careful when choosing topics. Some seemingly innocent topics can involve more paperwork than you would ever imagine. Take, for example, projects that include a student-prepared test or survey. This type of project involves human subjects. For projects involving human subjects, the ISEF rule book states, "All human research projects (including surveys, professional tests, questionnaires, and studies in which the researcher is the subject of his/her own research) are subject to a complete IRB review before experimentation begins."

Well, exactly what is required here? Clearly, a review of the student's proposed research by something called the IRB is necessary prior to the start of experimentation. The IRB, or Institutional Review Board, is a specially qualified group that can be in place at a research institution, school, or the regional/state science fair. The student must prepare a research plan that includes a copy of the proposed test, questionnaire, and so on. The student must also assess the risks to the subjects and state these risks in the informed consent form that is required for all projects involving human subjects. Because humans are the subject of the research, even though it may be a seemingly harmless survey, prior approval and informed consent releases signed by each survey participant will be needed for this project to compete at an ISEF-affiliated science fair.

Displays

The display that you bring to your science fair must comply with the rules of the ISEF if your fair is affiliated. Display and safety rules for the 1995 ISEF are summarized next.

Unacceptable for display: Living organisms; dried plant materials; taxidermy specimens or parts; preserved vertebrate or invertebrate animals, including embryos; human or animal food; human or animal parts except teeth, hair, nails, dried animal bones, histological dry-mount sections, and wet-mount tissue slides; soil or waste samples; chemicals including water, poisons, drugs, controlled substances, or hazardous substances or devices; dry ice or other sublimating solids; sharp items; flames or highly flammable display materials; empty tanks that previously contained combustible liquids or gases, unless purged with carbon dioxide; batteries with open top cells; awards, medals, business cards, flags, and other symbolic objects; and photographs or other visual presentations depicting vertebrate animals in other-than-normal conditions.

Acceptable for display but cannot be operated: Projects with unshielded belts, pulleys, chains, and moving parts with tension or pinch points; class III and IV lasers; and any device requiring over 110 volts.

Acceptable for display and operation with restrictions: Student-operated class II lasers; properly shielded large vacuum tubes or ray-generating devices; properly secured pressurized tanks that contain noncombustibles; adequately insulated apparatus producing harmful temperatures; and properly wired and insulated 110-volt AC circuits. See the ISEF rules for details about the restrictions to displays.

The size of display at the ISEF is limited to 30 inches (76 cm) deep by 48 inches (122 cm) wide and 108 inches (274 cm) high, including the height of the table.

Remember that these are the restrictions for competitors at the ISEF, and your local fair may do things differently. For sure, if you are the winner of a finalist slot to compete at the ISEF, you will have to make your project comply with its regulations.

During preliminary judging at the Connecticut Science Fair, when no students are present, we only allow student-built apparatus or models as part of the display. No electrical power is provided. We want each display to have its research report, laboratory notebooks, and other supporting materials that convey the scientific or engineering content of the student's work. In scientific meetings, this is known as a poster session. We are attempting to create a "level playing field" where creativity and scientific method are in the forefront. We chose this format to stop students from focusing on display "bells and whistles." Display wizardry was becoming the focal point for many students while the technical content was neglected or becoming, in some cases, an encyclopedic treatment of facts. We took a step beyond the rules of the ISEF to get the students and their advisors to concentrate on research. For our finalist judging with students present, we permit hardware that complies with the display rules.

This rule change has led to a sharp increase in the quality of the work. For instance, computers are now used for research *and* to generate display text and graphics. And by eliminating overly elaborate electronic presentations, the fair has been applauded by many science teachers and parents, who frequently comment that we have removed an element of financial bias from the competition.

Regardless of whether your local fair has such a rule, you should create a display that in your absence concisely describes your work and its significance.

Future Trends for Science Fairs

Team Projects

While many regional fairs have had team categories for many years, this is a new opportunity at the international level. Team projects, where a team of up to three students conduct the research, are a recent and significant change at the ISEF. Team activities reflect how work is accomplished in business and industry and are recognized by some educators as enhancing learning productivity. This latest ISEF category has a teamwork element in its judging criteria representing 16 percent of the score. Not all affiliated fairs send teams. Check this out if you're planning a team project with your sights on the ISEF.

Camcorder Science Fairs

Judging based on a time-limited video recording of the science project presented by the student is a venue that could become popular for the preliminary round of judging, if not the entire fair. It is an especially attractive technique for large states that lack a regional feeder fair structure.

Go for It!

From the many thousands of science projects prepared for local, regional, and state competition each year, 800 make it to the International Science and Engineering Fair. With a creative idea and good planning you will be off to a good start. It typically takes a few years to get your work to winning quality, so don't be discouraged. Learn from each project. I promise you that the experience you gain while doing a research project and communicating your results will serve you well in other endeavors.

Good luck! I hope to see your work at the ISEF someday.

George Robert Wisner
Chairman, Connecticut Science Fair Association, Inc.

ACKNOWLEDGMENTS

I would like to express my grateful appreciation to the many people who have touched my life by offering their support and assistance to make this revised edition possible. As with the first edition, I remain indebted to two wonderful people who selflessly continue to contribute so much of their time and talent to work with and encourage young students in science, mathematics, and engineering.

Special thanks are due George Robert Wisner, Chairman of the Connecticut Science Fair Association, Inc., and its Board of Directors, for graciously authoring the Foreword and offering his well-founded advice. Mr. Wisner is respected throughout the country for his successful orchestration of the Connecticut Science Fair as well as science fair workshops and scholarship opportunities for children. It has been a privilege to know and work with him over the past ten years.

At the same time, extra-special thanks are due Sister Mary Christine, Assistant Fair Director and member of the Board of Directors of the Connecticut Science Fair Association, for her assistance in selecting the 50 award-winning science fair projects that appear in Part Two. She also brightens the days of many students across the country who write me with queries about their science fair projects. As Chairman of the mathematics department at Mary Immaculate Academy in New Britain, Connecticut, Sister Mary Christine has mentored science students for almost 20 years.

Acknowledgment is also due Science Service, Inc., in Washington, D.C., for providing me with listings of the state, regional, and foreign science fairs. As a nonprofit institution, Science Service has been dedicated to providing education programs in science for students around the world since 1921.

I also wish to thank the people at John Wiley & Sons, Inc., who have made my job easier. Many thanks are due Kate Bradford, my editor, for her insight and for the opportunity to produce the revised edition, and to Kara Raezer, assistant editor, who dedicated her time as if the book were her own.

Finally, I wish to thank my parents, Edmund and Elizabeth Bochinski, who have always been there to support me.

Student Consultants

A very talented group of young scientists deserves an extra-special acknowledgment for their ideas and input into the science fair projects that appear in Part II. These students are:

- Eduardo Federico Canedo, "Does the Period of Motion of a Pendulum Depend on Its Weight, Amplitude, or Length?"
- Alexander Caravaca, "Does a Golf Ball's Bounciness Influence the Distance that It Will Travel?"
- Andrea Marie Caravaca, "Measuring the Brightness of an Incandescent Light Bulb"
- Hillary Charnas, "The Effects of Gender Identity on Short-Term Memory"
- George F. Claffey, "What Section of a Town Has the Most Pollution in the Form of Airborne Particles?"
- Amy Concilio, "What Colored Dyes Are Found in Powdered Drink Mix and Colored Marking Pens?"
- Brian J. Curtin, "Are Your Clams Safe to Eat?"
- Kirsten B. Glass, "How Effective Is Lobster Shell Chitin in Filtering Wastewater Metallic Ions?"
- Michelle Harris, "Polarization and Stress Analysis of Airplane Windows"
- Kristin Hertzig, "Are Dogs Colorblind?"
- Adam K. Horelik, "Do All Plants Transpire at the Same Rate Under Different Sources of Light?"
- Sara Horesco, "What Colored Dyes Are Found in Powdered Drink Mix and Colored Markers?"
- David A. Karanian, "The Relationship Between Alcohol Dosage and Dependency in a Rat"
- Albert Kim, "Which Angle of Attack Generates the Most Lift?"
- Theresa Konicki, "How Can the Amount of Bacteria Found on Kitchen Sponges and Dishcloths Be Reduced?"
- Iwona Korza, "The Great American Lawn and Pristine Water: Can They Coexist?"
- Kasia Koziol-Dube, "Can Food Molds Be Used to Reduce Bacteria Spread by a Pet Rabbit?"
- Cathy Magliocco, "Can Limestone Be Used to Protect Pine Trees from Acid Rain?"
- Jodi Marak, "How Does Acid Rain Affect the Cell Structure of *Spirogyra*?"
- Kathy Mikk, "How Does Saltwater Mix in an Estuary?"
- Meredith Miller, "The Effects of Gender Identity on Short-Term Memory"
- Christina L. Olson, "Environmental Effects on the Biodegradability of Plastic Bags, Paper Bags, and Newspaper"
- Sarah Ann Pacyna, "The Physics of Cheating in Baseball"

- Celeste N. Peterson, "Can the Heartbeat of a Chicken Embryo Be Detected Without Breaking Its Eggshell?"
- Mira Rho, "How Effective Are Various Items in Protecting Against Ultraviolet Radiation?"
- Jason Riha, "Are Composites of Wood Stronger than Solid Wood?"
- Laura Sharpe, "What Is The Effect of #6 Heating Oil on *Elodea densa* in an Aquatic Environment?"
- Christina Smilnak, "Can Plant Cloning Be Used Effectively by Produce Growers?"
- Robert Smith, "An Analysis of the Bacteria and Heavy Metal Content of Sewage Before and After Treatment at a Sewage Plant"
- Margaret Stanek, "How Effective Is Beta Carotene in Fighting Cancer in Plants?"
- Karen Thickman, "The Effect of Electromagnetic Fields on *Eremosphaera* Algae Cells"
- Connie W. Tsao, "Shape and Viscous Effect"
- Betsy Ruth Velasco, "What Substance Is Most Effective for Preventing the Breeding of Bacteria in Waterbeds?"
- Christopher Waluk, "Footwear versus Bacteria"
- Frank Waluk, "Can Earthworms Be Used to Recycle Kitchen Wastes into Fertile Garden Soil?" and "Are Dandelions as Effective as Commonly Prescribed Antibiotics against Bacteria?"
- John Wasielewski, "What Would Happen to Climate, Weather Patterns, and Life Forms if the Earth Were Cubical?"
- Joseph Wasielewski, "Can the Life Span of a Soap Bubble Be Extended in Different Temperatures and Atmospheric Conditions?" and "Can Mathematical Patterns Be Found in Johann Sebastian Bach's Two-Movement Preludes and Fugues?"
- Michael M. Wasielewski, "Do Gas Stations Affect the Soil Around Them?"

International Science and Engineering Fair Alumni

- Nicole D. D'Amato, "The Presence of Heavy Metals in a Coastal Body of Water and Their Effect on Aquatic Life"

- Matthew Green, "The Wave, the Golden Mean, and $r = \left[\dfrac{2}{\left(-1 + \sqrt{5} \right)} \right]^{\wedge} \theta$"

- Damon O. Kheir-Eldin, "Improving the Antibacterial Effects of Garlic"
- Katherine Frances Orzel, "The P-Trap: A Bacteria Cauldron" and "The P-Trap: A Continuing Dilemma"

SI (METRIC) CONVERSION TABLE

Both the English and the SI (metric) systems of measurement have been used in this book to simplify the student's understanding of specialized experimental procedures and the measurement-specific scientific instruments discussed.

	English	*Symbol* =	*SI (Metric)*	*Symbol*
Length	1 inch	in.	2.54 centimeters	cm
	1 foot	ft.	30.40 centimeters	cm
	1 yard	yd.	0.90 meter	m
	1 mile	mi.	1.60 kilometers	km
Mass	1 ounce	oz.	28.00 grams	g
	1 pound	lb.	0.45 kilogram	kg
Volume	1 teaspoon	tsp.	5.00 milliliters	ml
	1 tablespoon	tbsp.	15.00 milliliters	ml
	1 fluid ounce	fl. oz.	30.00 milliliters	ml
	1 cup	c.	0.24 liter	l
	1 pint	pt.	0.47 liter	l
	1 quart	qt.	0.95 liter	l
	1 gallon	gal.	3.80 liters	l

Temperature

Water freezes at:

32 degrees Fahrenheit	°F	0 degrees Celsius	°C

Water boils at:

212 degrees Fahrenheit		100 degrees Celsius	

Normal human body temperature:

98.6 degrees Fahrenheit		37 degrees Celsius	

To convert Fahrenheit to Celsius:

$$(°F - 32) \times \tfrac{5}{9}$$

To convert Celsius to Fahrenheit:

$$\frac{°C}{\tfrac{5}{9}} + 32$$

INTRODUCTION

It has been five years since the first edition of this book was published. During those years, I have received many kind letters and phone calls from students and teachers across the United States who found the first edition to be a helpful resource for guiding them through the science fair project process. I have also received correspondence from folks who brought inaccuracies to my attention and others who offered suggestions for improving parts of the book. I am grateful for all their comments and have incorporated many of their ideas in the new edition.

For every fan there is a critic, however, and with the praise has come a fair number of grievances and desperate cries for help from students who have brooded unsuccessfully over the outlines of the 50 sample science fair projects. There is something these students and you need to know, and I will try to break it to you gently: The project outlines are merely *recipes* that you are encouraged to *sample*, not *duplicate* in place of your own project. These projects have come from students like yourself and not from a lab textbook. Just because these projects have won awards does not mean that the outlines are guaranteed to work for you in accordance with the procedures given, nor are you guaranteed to win an award if you duplicate the same project. Please keep in mind that in order for a science project to have meaning for oneself and others, it may require additional testing, research, and adaptation to fully explore the question that is presented (see chapter 3). Nobody wins if a project is copied straight out of a book.

The science fair project outlines that appear in this book were included because they provide good examples of the methodology behind the scientific method (see chapter 1) after which you should model your project. Since many readers are first-time science fair participants who have never had the opportunity to visit a science fair to see what a science project looks like, the outlines are also a way to bring the science fair home to them. Additionally, for those students who are more experienced in science fair competition, the outlines show a range of skill and technique levels, from those used in simple projects to those used in sophisticated projects that have competed at the International Science and Engineering Fair (ISEF).

Science fairs have become an important key to gathering valuable science experience while you pursue an independent project of your choice. Every spring, over a million students like yourself participate in science fairs, from school-held fairs to the large regional fairs. And interest continues to grow. Since the 1980s, the number of science and engineering fairs in the United States and

Canada alone has nearly doubled. The reason for this boom is no surprise. Your generation was born during an era that has been labeled "the information age." Consequently, your generation is more fluent in technology than any other group of students that has come before you. In fact, many of you knew how to operate a personal computer before you even started school. As a result, your generation has become naturally curious about the effect of science on the world around you and is actively involved in performing science fair projects.

Science fairs are no longer considered to be sporting events for "propeller heads." Rather, they have become prestigious annual conventions for exchanging ideas and technologies between students of all interests and backgrounds. They are also a fun way to gather valuable science experience while pursuing a topic of interest to you. In many ways, they are your key to success and opportunity. In fact, many college recruiters rate science fair participation very highly.

Whether this is your first science fair project experience or whether you already have some experience, this book will introduce you to every aspect of science fairs and science fair projects. It will show you the shortcuts to finding a suitable topic, how to research it properly, how to develop an experiment, and how to give meaning to your data results. It will also give you guidelines and suggestions for an attractive display, together with tips for presenting your project to a panel of judges.

The second edition has been thoroughly updated to bring you as much current and useful information as possible. Once again, this edition contains 50 award-winning science fair project outlines. Changes have been made, however, to improve upon the procedures found in many of the outlines, and ten new and exciting project outlines replace outlines that have caused difficulty for students. This edition also contains a new chapter, chapter 7, which discusses, in depth, the makings of a successful research project from the germination of an idea through four years of experimentation.

The appendixes have also been revised. Appendix A has been greatly improved to include 400 workable science fair project topics, while Appendixes B and C have been thoroughly updated to bring you, respectively, 40 excellent science supply sources across the United States and a list of state, regional, and foreign affiliates of the ISEF. Appendix D, which is new, was added to give you information about alternative science fair competitions in which you can enter your work.

In the past three years, much has changed at the regional science fair level. New rules have been implemented to govern the protocol a student must follow before attempting to perform certain forms of scientific research and to serve as guidelines on what can be displayed at a science fair. These changes were instituted in 1993 by the ISEF for its affiliated regional fairs. I have left the formidable task of translating these new rules and guidelines into plain English to my longtime friend and mentor, George Robert Wisner, Chairman of the Connecticut Science Fair Association. He has explained these changes in the Foreword, where he also offers a good deal of practical advice for students, parents, and teachers. I strongly urge you to read this section.

I hope you will find this "new and improved" edition to be your chief resource as you make your way through the process of completing and submitting a science fair project. By using this book, you should find your science fair project easier to organize and present and your work more meaningful. I hope your weeks and months of hard work will be rewarded by your project being selected as a finalist and an award winner. But most of all, I hope that you will gain useful experience in a particular scientific field and will someday contribute by means of that experience to the scientific community.

PART

1

A Complete Guide to Science Fair Projects

1

SCIENCE FAIRS AND SCIENCE FAIR PROJECTS

What Is a Science Fair?

Every year, during the spring season, thousands of students in junior and senior high school prepare science fair projects for science fairs. Many schools present science fairs after their students have completed a group of science projects. These fairs are public exhibitions of the students' projects to provide recognition for their work and to stimulate interest in science. Professionals from the scientific community often judge the science projects according to commonly accepted scientific standards.

If you participate in a science fair you may compete for prizes and for the chance to move on to a higher competition in a state or regional fair, or to the highest level in the International Science and Engineering Fair (ISEF), considered to be the "Super Bowl" of science fairs. One of the most important aspects of science fairs is that they give you educational opportunities for exchanging and learning new scientific methods and concepts with professionals and other contestants. (See Appendix C for a complete listing of state, regional, and foreign fairs affiliated with the ISEF.) Since most state and regional science fairs, along with their school and town feeder fairs, subscribe to rules and guidelines established by the ISEF, this book will prepare you for such fairs.

What Is a Science Fair Project?

A science fair project gives you the opportunity to gain hands-on experience and knowledge in an independent field of study. It is a challenging, extracurricular assignment that allows you to use your own ideas or a topic provided by your instructor to investigate scientific problems that interest you.

The Scientific Method

It seems only fair to set forth the component parts of a science fair project by giving you a few definitions before you plan your first project.

Each year, thousands of students enter state, regional, or foreign affiliates of the International Science and Engineering Fair.

A science project is your attempt to study a scientific problem in order to answer a proposed question or develop a better technique or final product. Science projects primarily involve research and tests to arrive at a specific conclusion. The basic procedure involved in science projects is modeled on a process

A science fair project is modeled after a system called the scientific method.

called **the scientific method**. This method consists of the following elements: purpose, hypothesis, research, experiment, and conclusion. Each element may be defined as follows:

Purpose. The problem or question for which you are seeking a solution. *(Example: Does an interrupted sleeping pattern affect alertness?)*

Hypothesis. Your educated guess about the solution to the question. *(Example: I believe that sleep influences one's alertness.)*

Research. The process by which you gather information by consulting libraries, instructors, professionals, or scientific organizations. Also, the period for planning and organizing your experiment.

Experiment. The process by which you develop your subject knowledge and research findings into tests. *(Example: Two groups of people will be studied. Group I will be allowed to sleep 9 hours without interruption. Group II will be allowed to sleep 10 hours but will be awakened every 2 hours for 15 minutes to give group members a total of 9 hours of sleep. Following the periods of sleep, both groups will be tested for alertness to determine whether their performance is influenced by the conditions they were subjected to prior to the test.)*

Conclusion. The solution to your proposed question and proof or disproof of your hypothesis. *(Example: Based on the data from this test, interrupted sleepers perform less efficiently than noninterrupted ones on a standard alertness test.)*

2
GETTING STARTED

Select a Topic

Believe it or not, selecting a topic for a science project is the toughest part of the process for some students. Every year many students who plan to do a science fair project begin the usual public library search through volumes and volumes of scientific literature without knowing what they are looking for. After several useless attempts at finding information, most students end up quitting in frustration. The public library is not a bad place to find a topic; in fact, it is a very good place; but most students are not organized when they begin their search for a topic.

Think About Your Interests

The first step in getting organized is picking an area of science in which you have some particular interest or experience. One suggestion is to make a list of general science categories that you like. Then, go through your list and classify each category into subcategories of interest. For example, if one of the categories you listed was *health*, some subcategories might include *nutrition*, *diet*, and *vitamins*. Chances are good that you will find yourself more interested in one area than in another. Such preferences usually indicate good possibilities for topics. If, for example, you chose *vitamins* as your subject, you should then try to identify a particular aspect of vitamins that you want to investigate. Do you want to study the effects a particular vitamin has in alleviating arthritis, or do you want to see how it functions as a supplement with certain foods? If you chose *birds* as your subject, you should determine whether you want to study the atmospheric conditions that influence their migration, or to see how atmospheric conditions affect their life span. These are just a few examples of how you would develop a topic from your selected subject area. For a list of 400 science project topic suggestions, see Appendix A.

Remember that your best choice for a topic is a subject in which you have a particular interest. While it is helpful to have some knowledge of the topic before you choose it, this is not essential. If you are interested and resourceful, you will learn what you need to know. Remember, there is nothing worse than to be unhappy with your topic. Don't be afraid to get out of it and find another topic if you do happen to become bored or disinterested with your original choice.

Think About Your Experiences

Another means of selecting a topic is examining your past experiences. Ask yourself whether you remember any unusual experiences in your life. For example, perhaps you once felt that your eyesight improved whenever you ate a certain vegetable, or perhaps you discovered a rare type of moss growing on a tree stump in your backyard. You may have wondered whether the material that enabled your watch dial to glow in the dark also emitted radiation that was affecting your environment. Personal experiences such as these are excellent sources for project ideas.

Research Science Abstracts

Another possible source for a good topic is scientific abstracts. Abstracts can be located in bound scientific journals that are usually available at your local college or university libraries. These specialized journals are used primarily by science professionals. Articles are generally grouped into two classes: research experimental reports and reviews of scientific literature. Monthly issues are published in accordance with a cumulative subject and author index that is published annually.

Research Periodicals

Another area to investigate if you have not already thought of a topic is the periodicals in your field of interest. Go to your local library and look through the most recent magazines and newsletters in the field you have chosen. These are effective aids in finding and researching a topic because they are concise and up to date. Magazines such as *National Geographic, Discover, Popular Science, Popular Mechanics, Mother Earth News, Scientific American, High Technology,* and *Prevention Health Magazine* are some of the best journals to consult while searching for an original topic.

Research Current Topics

Keep in mind, too, that a successful project tends to be one that employs a new technology, current issue, or novel approach. For example, in the late 1970s and early 1980s, the main public concern of many Americans was the energy issue, so projects that involved energy themes fared well. Today, environmental issues are popular. You can often find topics on the latest issues by reading periodical journals and scientific abstracts.

Visit a Local or Regional Science Fair

One of the best ways to get ideas is to surround yourself with them. If you are still having trouble finding a science fair project topic, try visiting a local school or regional science fair. Not only will you be able to see the quality of science work performed by junior and senior high school students, but you will also be able to see what topics are current and interesting to you.

Read This Book

If you cannot visit a local or regional fair, you can get ideas for a topic from this book. For your convenience, this book contains the outlines of 50 award-winning projects, including several projects that were candidates in the ISEF. The outlines describe the materials these finalists used, their objectives, and the experimental procedures they followed. The actual findings were left out and questions were added in their place, so that you may use these projects as models and draw your own conclusions. The projects were not intended to do the work for you, but rather to give you an idea of how topics can be developed.

Organize Your Investigation

Once you have found a topic that satisfies you, you are ready to get started. At this time, it is necessary to reorganize yourself and take inventory. You can begin by getting a notebook to create a journal of everything that you will be learning and doing on your project. A journal often proves to be the most efficient way of organizing your research, and what's more, it will serve as an excellent outline for your report. Describe in your journal articles you have read, places you have visited, data results, and other points you think are worth noting. Write down important information so that you will not have to search through past references again.

As a researcher, you are investigating a particular problem or question. It would be helpful to know exactly what you are aiming for and how far you are willing to go to pursue your immediate objective. Before you get started, take into consideration the amount of time you have to complete the project, plan it accordingly, and—most importantly—find out if certain conditions limit you or your topic.

Project Limitation Guidelines

Rules established by the ISEF will govern your research and experimentation. In 1993, the ISEF's Scientific Review Committee rewrote its rules out of concern for the safety and protection of student researchers and their advisors, as well as to comply with local and federal regulations governing research. Some of the areas in which strict rules apply involve vertebrate and nonvertebrate animals, human subjects, recombinant DNA, human and animal tissues, pathogenic agents, controlled substances, and hazardous material or devices. For projects involving those areas, you are now required to complete additional forms and have them approved by an institutional review board at your state or regional science fair prior to the start of research. Please read the Foreword for a review and discussion of the new rules, or contact your state or regional fair director. A copy of the ISEF rule book can be obtained from Science Service, Inc., 1719 N Street, N.W., Washington, D.C. 20036.

Begin Your Research

A good way to begin work on your topic is by checking all relevant periodicals and scientific abstracts at your library. Most current scientific articles list additional sources of cross-references at the end of their reports. Some give the names and addresses of organizations and people who can supply more information, such as area groups, universities, or technicians. Take advantage of these helpful references because they are your best source for up-to-date facts.

As soon as you think you have located some useful addresses, write a letter to the organization or person mentioned in the article or cross-reference. State that you are a student working under a deadline, and discuss the plans you have in mind for your project and the information you will need to gather. Ask for all available literature and any suggestions for experimentation. Also, ask for additional references of persons in your area who are working in this field.

Make several copies of this letter and send them to the people and organizations who may be able to help you. Most people will be glad to help, especially if it relates to their own ideas or products. Sending out such letters enables you to save time by eliminating useless searches and limiting your information to the details that you need. Remember, you can always refer to textbooks, periodicals, and scientific abstracts when you need additional information.

Printed below are two letters. One was sent out by a student requesting information on alcohol as an alternative energy resource. This letter resulted in four informational guides that helped the student through her entire project. Along with the guides, she received lists containing the titles of exclusive literature on her subject and the address of an alcohol fuel producer who lived in her own county. The other was sent out by another student requesting information on testing corked baseball bats. This letter helped the student make contact with a helpful advisor.

Renewable Energy Information
P.O. Box 8900
Silver Spring, MD 20907

Dear Director:

I am a high school student currently working on a science project for the Connecticut Science Fair. My project concerns the recycling of fermented organic garbage into ethyl alcohol. My objective is to see if it is possible for a household to construct a simple and inexpensive still capable of producing enough alcohol fuel to meet the household's energy needs. I also plan to compare ethyl alcohol with other natural fuel sources to determine its efficiency.

(Continued)

Recently, I found your address in an alcohol fuel directory. This guide mentioned that your organization would be able to assist ethyl alcohol fuel producers by providing them with suggestions and further information.

At this time, I would be grateful for any current information on alcohol production, still designs, and alcohol producers in my area. If possible, please send this information to me soon since I am working toward a February deadline.

If all goes well, this will be both an informative and stimulating project for me and my community.

Sincerely,

Student

February 1, 1992
Hillerich & Bradsby Company
P.O. Box 35700
Louisville, KY 40232-5700

Dear Sir:

I am an eighth grade student in Connecticut. In January, I won first place at my school science fair and will be going on to the State Science Fair on March 9, 1992.

My project topic was "The Physics of Cheating in Baseball." Four bats were used to test my hypothesis which was that a baseball bat filled with sawdust, as opposed to a regular bat or bats filled with cork or rubber balls, will cause a baseball to travel the farthest on impact. I drilled out the center of three bats and filled one with sawdust, the second with rolled cork and the third with rubber balls. I left one bat alone to serve as a control. I tested the bats by placing each of them in a swinging device which would hit a baseball placed on a batting tee when released. Out of the four bats, the sawdust-filled bat sent the baseball farther than the other bats.

In preparation for the State Science Fair, I would like to expand my project by seeing if it is possible to X-ray a baseball bat. I spoke with my doctor to find out if he or someone else would be willing to perform the X rays. He told me that I would have to find out whether a Diagnostic Machine X ray or Metal Fatigue/ Stress Fracture X ray would have to be performed. Please tell me which of these X rays would work with baseball bats.

Also, in doing my research I read an article, "The Physics of Foul Play" in *Discover*, April 1988, in which tests were conducted in 1987 at the request of Peter Ueberroth. Do you have any information on how the bats were tested and what the results were? I would appreciate having this information as soon as possible since I am working under a limited time frame. Thank you for your assistance.

Sincerely,

Sarah A. Pacyna

Summary

1. Select a topic by focusing on an area that interests you and by identifying a specific category for a project.

2. Identify what you are looking for and how far you are willing to go to pursue your immediate objective. (This includes checking with your advisor and reviewing the ISEF regulations. See the Foreword and/or contact Science Service, the administrator of the ISEF, for a copy of the rules.)

3. Create a journal of important points in your research.

4. Research periodicals and scientific abstracts for cross-references and addresses to contact organizations or persons in your subject area.

5. Write a letter and send copies of it to each of the groups you have selected.

3

CONDUCTING
AN EXPERIMENT

The experiment can either make or break your science project. This is the back-bone of the project, and it is essential that you put sufficient thought and prepara-tion into it. Thus, you should plan to spend most of your time on a feasible experiment after researching. After all, this is where you contribute your own ideas and creative ability.

Your experiment should encompass everything that you have learned about your topic. Your research should be applied to a practical application that involves measurements, analyses, or tests to answer a specific question. Judges look for these individual qualities and will be distracted if your project contains irrelevant facts and data.

Make sure that the work you do is an experiment. Judges all too often see projects that are researched thoroughly and presented in a neat, attractive manner, only to find a presentation of a well-known idea or a display that the public has seen

The experiment is perhaps the most important part of a science fair project.

too many times. Such exhibits are not experiments but mere demonstrations. While preparing your project, try to present a question and then prepare a series of tests to solve the problem or support a proposed hypothesis. If you follow the scientific method (see chapter 1), your project should be easier to complete and will provide more meaningful results than if you do not use this method.

Because you will want your results to be absolutely accurate, you should record all your data, regardless of whether or not they support your hypothesis. Your project will not be scored low or disqualified simply because your results did not support your hypothesis. You may develop your project by interpreting your end results and explaining why they were different than what you had expected.

Keep in mind that judges do not expect you to come up with a revolutionary idea. They are more interested in seeing how much scientific skill and thought you applied to your project. Most projects have been done before in one form or another. They usually differ to the extent that they are applied techniques of an original idea or a confirmation of a conclusion under varying circumstances. Some contestants even submit the same project in a following science fair because they have made significant progress in their topics since their first entry.

Define Your Objective

Before you begin, it is essential that you streamline your proposed question. Decide what it is that you want to prove, and try to attack the most important aspect of your topic. For example, if you chose toxic waste as your topic, you would probably research its hazardous byproducts, clean-up solutions, and future outlook. Such a broad topic would yield a variety of details without a specific focus or purpose. It should be clear that you must confine your topic to a single purpose or question. This can be done by listing all the different approaches that may be taken in your project through experimentation. Some of these might include:

1. Determining the effects that industrially contaminated waste has on the growth of organisms.
2. Comparing health and disease statistics between different toxic waste sites.
3. Determining the efficiency of a proposed solution to neutralize toxic waste.

After you have listed various approaches to your project, choose one that you think will produce a reasonable and practical experiment.

Given these choices, the second alternative would probably be too broad to work with. Such an experiment would require several years in order for you to compare the health and disease characteristics of several sites. The work would involve periodic studies of people, animals, and plants, in order to measure their endurance, immunity, and quality of vital functions. Although this is a very challenging idea, it might be too general to satisfy your immediate objective. The third alternative would be a great experiment if you had access to a new toxic waste solution, such as a chemical that would act as a stabilizer in eliminating byproducts. You could measure the efficiency of this chemical in order to find out which byproducts it could break down. However, this project would be too diverse to satisfy your immediate objective and would pose a problem if you did not already have a solution in mind.

The first topic probably would be the best choice, because it focuses on one central idea—the effects of toxic waste on growth. A procedural plan could easily be developed to parallel your purpose.

Organize Your Experiment

Once you have reduced your topic to a single purpose or question, you must organize your experiment. In the example regarding toxic waste, you must organize an experiment that will allow you to measure growth in the presence of industrially contaminated waste. It would be difficult to measure human or animal growth in a short time period, so a more practical subject would be a plant. Since you may not detect any noticeable difference in growth by merely placing the plant in the presence of toxic waste, you may decide instead to place the plant (*Coleus*, for example) in various samples of contaminated soil from different manufacturing and dumping sites. Your objective would then be to study the effects of toxic soil on the growth of a *Coleus* plant. After you have organized your experiment, a procedural plan must be developed.

Create a Procedural Plan

A procedural plan is a uniform, systematic way of testing your hypothesis. Such testing requires that you first correlate what you want to prove. Correlation is done with two or more variables—dependent and independent. The dependent variable is the one that is being measured; the independent variable is the one that is controlled or manipulated by the experiment. For example, you may want to see whether the health and growth of a tomato plant (the dependent variable) is influenced by the amount of light the plant is exposed to (the independent variable). Several other independent variables may be used instead, such as water, oxygen, carbon dioxide, nitrogen levels, etc. However, for the sake of clarity we will use only light as a variable for this example.

Establish a Control Group

Next, an experimental group and a control group must be established. The control group provides you with a basis for comparing the experimental group. For example, you may have an experimental group of tomato plants which is placed in a sunny window for two weeks and watered periodically. At the end of the period, the plants have grown three inches and are very green. At this point, you may conclude that sunlight does indeed increase plant growth. But before you draw this conclusion, you should determine whether the tomato plants would have grown and become green without any sunlight at all. This is where a control group of plants is needed.

The control group of plants would be those that are given the same treatment as the experimental ones, with the exception that they not be exposed to sunlight. If the outcome of the experiment was that there was a significant difference between the two groups, then you probably would be justified in concluding that tomato plant growth is influenced by the amount of sunlight the plant receives.

The procedural plan in this example is very simple, but it gives you an idea of the process of an experiment. In essence, the procedural plan advances from one stage to another in an organized fashion. Remember, however, that most experiments are not as simple as the one described here. Often, obstacles arise and other interesting characteristics of the subject are revealed in the process. You may even discover existing differences in several trials with only one variable. In fact, this is a frequent occurrence, and it is an important reason why you must keep accurate data records (see chapter 4).

How to Avoid a Failed Experiment

There are several reasons why an experiment may fail to validate a hypothesis, prove a point, or simply do what it was intended to do. Such reasons include: mistakes in the way the experiment was carried out (procedural errors), a poor or incomplete final analysis, and erroneous hypotheses.

Procedural Errors

To avoid procedural problems, you must perform regular and consistent maintenance on your subject and controls. For example, in the experiment involving sunlight and tomato plants, if you gave the experimental group of tomato plants more water than the control group or planted them in a soil that contained more nitrogen, you would get artificial results. This means that you are failing to control or hold your variable constant. How can you determine whether it was the sunlight alone or in combination with other factors that made the experimental tomatoes flourish? The same problem with inconsistent maintenance of controls might apply if you were studying the behavior of your friends at a party for a psychological experiment. What would happen if you made your study obvious by taking notes and pictures? Your friends probably would be influenced by your behavior and would not act in their usual manner. These examples involve manipulated experiments that would yield useless data. Of course, there are other procedural problems that arise during an experiment, especially if poorly calibrated measuring instruments are used.

Poor Final Analysis

Even after a carefully controlled experiment is completed, errors can still occur. Such errors could result from an incorrect analysis of results. For example, if you concluded that a certain salve cures acne, on the basis of tests that were conducted on female adolescents but not male ones, your final analysis would be inconclusive. While the salve may have worked on the females you tested, it may not work on females in different age groups or on males of all age groups. Other problems with final analysis may arise from mathematical errors or from data that are irrelevant to the topic.

Erroneous Hypotheses

When an experiment is completed, the results are sometimes quite different from those that were predicted. If this occurs, do not manipulate the results to fit the initial hypothesis. Often, it may be that the hypothesis was incorrect or vague and that the experimental results were accurate. If such problems occur in your project, you can salvage your work by finding out why the results were different than expected or by explaining a new or unexpected observation or solution. This will show the judges that you remained interested and involved in the subject matter.

Keep in mind that many scientific investigations do not support their specific goals. However, this does not weaken the validity of their conclusions. In fact, many experiments require additional testing and exploration to understand a particular phenomenon. Sometimes, unexpected experimental results lead to surprising discoveries and more interesting science projects!

Summary

1. The experiment is an essential part of your science project. It should test, survey, compare, and ultimately examine the validity of your hypothesis.
2. You must focus your topic on an experimental approach that will clearly test your hypothesis.
3. After you decide on an experimental approach, you must organize a procedural plan.
4. A procedural plan is a uniform, systematic way of testing a subject.
5. An experimental group and a control group must be established as part of the procedural plan.
6. Three common ways in which an experiment can fail are: procedural errors, poor final analysis, and erroneous hypotheses.

4

ORGANIZING AND PRESENTING DATA

A vital part of the scientific method is being able to explain your data and what you have learned to others. Since you began your experiment, you have been gathering data. Data are essentially groups of figures for a given experiment. During the initial stages of an experiment, they may have little meaning, so it is important that you compile and organize your data accurately for your final analysis, observations, and conclusions. A good way to keep data is to record them in your project journal. After you have written down all the experimental results in an organized way, you can easily refer to your results to make generalizations and conclusions. There are several methods of presenting data, including the basic tabular, graphic, and statistical methods.

Tabulating and Graphing

As mentioned, raw data have little or no meaning in and of themselves. It is only when they are organized into tabular and graphic forms that they can be understood in terms of a scientific method or objective. The data results must be grasped quickly and correctly by the observer, so that he or she can see the project in a coherent perspective. Tables are relatively simple to make and form the basis for most graphs. The main points to consider are organization and coordination. For example, consider these recordings in tabular form of the body temperature of a flu patient:

Times	Body Temperature (°F)
6:00 A.M.	97.0
8:00 A.M.	98.0
10:00 A.M.	99.0
Noon	100.0
2:00 P.M.	101.0
4:00 P.M.	102.0
6:00 P.M.	103.0
8:00 P.M.	102.0
10:00 P.M.	100.0
Midnight	98.0

If you want to see how the patient's temperature fluctuated during the day, you can do this by looking at the table. But if you want to see at a glance how the patient's temperature changed, a graphic representation would be more effective.

A line graph may be used for this analysis. A line graph is comprised of two axes: the x, or horizontal, and the y, or vertical. The x axis contains all the points for one set of data, and the y axis contains all the points for the other set of data.

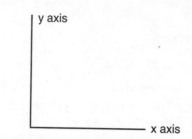

For example, you could label a range of body temperatures on the y axis and label the times on the x axis. After your axes are labeled, simply plot the points. Plotting involves matching each temperature with the corresponding time and marking them on the graph. For example, at 6:00 A.M. the body temperature was 97 degrees Fahrenheit, so you should locate and mark the point on the x and y axes at which 6:00 A.M. and 97 degrees correspond. Then do this for the rest of the data and connect the dots to complete the curve.

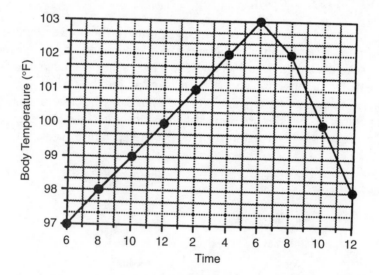

From this graph, one can quickly see that the patient's body temperature rose gradually, peaked late in the day, and fell during the evening.

Another means of graphical representation that makes data easily understandable is the pie chart. Suppose that you are testing a specimen of blood to determine the percentage of its composition of erythrocytes, leukocytes, and thrombocytes. After several tests and microscopical observation you conclude that the blood contained the percentages as shown in the following table:

Cell Type	% Composition
Erythrocytes	50.0%
Thrombocytes	38.0%
Leukocytes	12.0%
	Σ* = 100.0%

*Σ is a Greek symbol that means "the summation of."

The data can be represented in a pie chart:

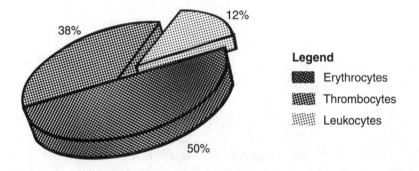

Each section represents a percentage of the pie. It is easy to see that the leukocyte blood count is low in terms of its percentage of the total composition.

There are many other ways to graph your data besides the two methods shown. The important thing to remember about graphing is that it summarizes your results in a visual form that emphasizes the differences between groups of data results. As the old saying goes, a picture is worth a thousand words.

The Statistical Method

Some very simple statistics will allow you to expand on your data. Some of these applications include: the *mean, frequency distribution*, and *percentile*.

The **mean**, expressed as $\bar{x}$, where x is any rational number, is a mathematical average that is really the central location of your data. The sum of your data numbers is denoted by the symbol Σ, which means "the summation of." This sum is then divided by the quantity of your data recordings, which is the symbol n. Thus, the mean is expressed as this formula:

$$\bar{x} = \frac{\Sigma x}{n}$$

For example, consider the mean fluoride level in parts per million (ppm) from 11 different water departments.

Town Name	Fluoride Level (ppm)
A-Town	1.00
B-Town	1.50

C-Town	1.50
D-Town	0.05
E-Town	0.04
F-Town	1.01
G-Town	0.09
H-Town	0.05
I-Town	2.00
J-Town	1.00
K-Town	1.00

$$\Sigma(x) = 9.24$$

Using the formula, you can express your results as follows: If $\Sigma(x) = 9.24$ and $n = 11$, then $\bar{x} = 9.24/11 = 0.8400$. The figure 0.8400 is the mean, or the mathematical average of the studied water plants.

Now suppose that you collected samples from 50 water plants. It may be difficult to generalize about the results, so a better method is needed to record the data. One way of describing the results statistically is with a **frequency distribution**. This method is a summary of a set of observations showing the number of items in several categories. For example, suppose that the following levels were observed to be present in 50 samples:

Fluoride Levels (ppm)	Frequency (f)
2.00	3
1.70	6
1.50	7
1.00	8
0.90	10
0.80	7
0.05	6
0.04	3
	$\Sigma f = 50n$

These results can be graphed using a histogram which represents your frequency distribution. With a histogram, your item classes are placed along the horizontal axis and your frequencies along the vertical axis. Then, rectangles are drawn with the item classes as the bases and frequencies as the sides. This type of diagram is useful because it clearly shows that the fluoride levels are normally at the 0.90 to 1.00 ppm mark (see diagram on next page).

The **percentile** is another useful statistic. A percentile is the position of one value from a set of data that expresses the percentage of the other data that lie below this value. To calculate the position of a particular percentile, first put the values in ascending order. Then, divide the percentile you want to find by 100 and

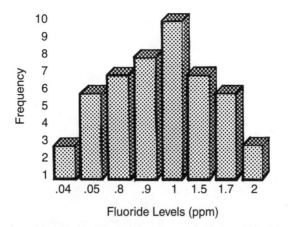

Fluoride Levels (ppm)

multiply by the number of values in the data set. If the answer is not an integer (a positive or negative whole number), round up to the next position of the data value you're looking for. If the answer is an integer, average the data values of that position and the next higher one for the data value you're looking for. For example, suppose that you wanted to test the efficiency of 11 automobiles by measuring how many miles each car gets to a gallon of gasoline. You have recorded the following data: 17.6, 16.4, 18.6, 16.1, 16.3, 15.9, 18.9, 19.7, 19.1, 20.2, and 19.5. First you would arrange the numbers in ascending order: 15.9, 16.1, 16.3, 16.4, 17.6, 18.6, 18.9, 19.1, 19.5, 19.7, and 20.2. Now suppose that you want to determine which car ranked in the 90th percentile. To calculate the 90th percentile for this data set, write this equation: $(90/100)(11) = 9.9$. Since 9.9 is not an integer, round up to 10, and the tenth value is your answer. The tenth value is 19.7; therefore, the car that traveled 19.7 miles per gallon of gasoline is in the 90th percentile, and 90% of the cars in your study were less gas efficient.

In summary, you will have to decide which tabular and graphical technique works best for your type of data. You can usually express your results in terms of either standard mathematical or statistical graphing. However, there are occasions when only one type will work. If you are dealing with numerous figures or classes of figures, a statistical graph usually works best. For example, if you wanted to demonstrate the variation of test scores between boys and girls in the eighth grade, you would probably make your point clearer by using the statistical method, which would allow you to find the percentiles in which each student scored and the mean test score. On the other hand, if you were investigating the mineral composition of water, the best way to represent the proportion of its contents would be through a pie chart.

Summary

1. Data are recorded information that are organized for final analysis and observation.
2. The basic tabular, basic graphic, and statistical methods are some of the basic ways of presenting data.

5

THE DISPLAY

The display is an essential part of your project. Although it alone will not save a bad project, it can enhance the success of a good one. There is nothing more disappointing than to have a judge or viewer overlook a meritable project purely on the basis of its illegible or disorganized display. Therefore, it is worth spending some extra time making an attractive display.

Due to the guidelines established by the International Science and Engineering Fair, most state and regional fairs have put emphasis on a "poster session" approach, where the backboard is the focal point of the display. Therefore, your display should consist of a report and a backboard containing tables, graphs, charts, photographs, and diagrams.

Your exhibit should display all aspects of your project. There are many ways to do this, but you must remember that all information should be self-explanatory. Lengthy discussions should be confined to the report.

An attractive display can enhance a project's success.

Most state and regional fairs have put emphasis on a "poster session" approach where the backboard is the focal point of the display.

The Backboard

The backboard is usually the most important part of your display. It should include all the major parts of your project. The backboard is essentially an upright, self-supporting board with organized highlights of your project. It is usually three-sided, although it does not necessarily have to be. The backboard should meet the spacing standards of the ISEF if you plan to enter your project in a state or regional fair that is affiliated with the ISEF. The dimensions of your project must not exceed 108 inches (274 cm) in height, 30 inches (76 cm) in depth and 48 inches (122 cm) in width. If these dimensions are exceeded, you may be disqualified.

When constructing your backboard, it is a good idea to stay away from posterboard or cardboard. Backboards made of these materials tend to bend and do not look very professional. It may be worth your while to purchase a firm, self-supporting material such as corkboard, pegboard, or reinforced paperboard. In the long run, you will find these types of materials easier to work with and more attractive.

Select appropriate lettering for your backboard. You might even want to purchase self-sticking letters or make use of the services of a professional printer. In recent years, many students have produced attractive backboard lettering by means of a word processor attached to a laser printer. Because there are so

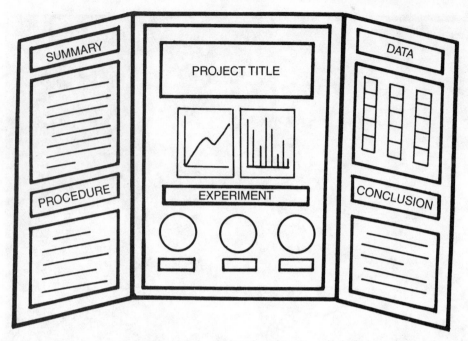

The information on your backboard should be placed in an orderly fashion from left to right under organized headings.

many lettering options available today, there is little reason to handprint your backboard.

Now that you know how to construct a backboard, you need to know what information you should put on it and where to place it. There is no standard way of making a backboard; however, all the information displayed on it should be well organized. The project title, for example, should stand out in the middle section in bold print. The rest of your information should be placed in an orderly fashion from left to right under organized headings. Some students even like to use the steps of the scientific method as their headings. Others apply headings that relate more specifically to their subject. Whatever headings you choose, make sure they are explicit and follow a format. After you plan out your format you can fill in extra spaces with additional visual information on your subject.

The information that you place under each heading is crucial. It must be concise and inclusive. Do not fill up your backboard with excess information. Try to summarize the facts under each heading in no more than 300 words.

The Report

It is also important that your report be of good quality. This means that you must organize a portfolio of clearly stated, factual information. It is important to keep this in mind because the report is essentially your spokesperson when you are not with your project.

An organized report contains the historical background on your subject, an introduction that states your purpose, a procedure that explains your means of acquiring information, your plan for organizing an experiment, and all the recorded data, diagrams, photos, conclusions, and other details that fully explain your project. You might even want to include detailed descriptions about different phases in your experiment in the form of a diary. It is a good idea to include the names and places you have visited, together with any related correspondence.

Your report may in fact be easier to complete if you create a journal (see chapter 2). If you record everything as you go along, all you will need to do later is organize your notes, because your journal is essentially your report.

In organizing your report, you will have to distinguish between primary and secondary sources of information. Primary sources of information consist of surveys, observations, and experimentations that you have done. Secondary sources are outside sources, such as the library, media organizations, government agencies, and companies. If you have used secondary sources for information either quoted directly or used indirectly, you must acknowledge these sources in footnotes and in a bibliography.

Be sure to type or print the final draft of your report. A report will not be able to explain your project as well as you can, but it is reassuring to know that an organized and professional report can work well for you in your absence.

You should remember that if you write a thorough report that encompasses all the items mentioned here, you may be eligible to submit it to another type of science competition also, such as the Westinghouse Science Talent Search or a local Junior Science and Humanities Symposium. For more information on these types of competitions, see Appendix D.

The Abstract

An abstract is a brief summary of your project that is about 250 words long. The abstract explains the project's purpose and procedural plan and presents generalized data and a short discussion of your conclusions. There is no standard way to write an abstract, but it should always be brief and well written.

Some science fairs require that their finalists submit an abstract on judging day. A useful thing to do is to write your abstract in advance in order to avoid leaving out any necessary information. Even though the abstract does not affect your score or influence your final status, it is usually kept on record by your state science fair for future reference, and it may even be read by a special award sponsor.

Display Restrictions

You read in chapter 2 about the project limitation guidelines established by the ISEF. The ISEF also has strict regulations involving the exhibition of certain articles in conjunction with the rest of your exhibit. Please read the Foreword and/ or contact Science Service, the administrator of the ISEF, for more information about what is acceptable for display.

A rule of thumb is to avoid anything that could be potentially hazardous to display in public. You can usually uphold such regulations by using photographs and model simulations. As always, however, if you have any doubts about displaying any part of your subject, be sure to first check with officials from your local science fair or contact the ISEF.

Summary

1. The display of your science project must be presented in an organized and attractive manner.
2. The display should consist of a report and a backboard containing tables, graphs, charts, photographs, and diagrams.
3. Backboards must meet the standard space requirements established by the ISEF, which are 108 inches (274 cm) in height, 30 inches (76 cm) in depth, and 48 inches (122 cm) in width.
4. The report can be created primarily from a journal, but it should be organized around primary and secondary sources of information.
5. An abstract is a short essay that summarizes the goals, methods, and conclusions of your project.
6. The ISEF has established regulations for the restriction and modification of potentially hazardous items for display.

6
AT THE FAIR

This chapter will prepare you for what lies ahead. If you follow the format for completing a project that is recommended here, you should be successful. All that you need to be concerned with at this time is reserving a spot for your project and registering in the correct category.

At some state and regional fairs there are only two broad categories in which you may register—**biological sciences** and **physical sciences** (although there are several divisions within each of these categories that are designated by grade levels). The biological sciences category consists of projects that pertain to the life sciences, including behavioral sciences, biochemistry, botany, ecology, genetics, medicine and health, microbiology, zoology, animal species studies, disease studies, etc. The physical sciences category consists of projects that encompass chemistry, math, earth sciences, space science, engineering, physics, toxic waste studies, electronics, and so on.

It is usually easy to determine where your project belongs, but sometimes it may be difficult. For example, if you did a project on prosthetic devices, in which you studied the physics of how artificial joints wear after a period of time, in what category would your project belong? If your project emphasized the amount of

Your backboard should be self-supporting, but it is wise to bring glue, tape, and a stapler for minor repairs.

friction in a joint, it would probably be a physical sciences project. But, if you began to discuss the biodegradability of the device, your project might be more appropriately placed in the biological sciences category. The wrong choice could hurt your outcome in the competition.

As you set up your project, pay careful attention to the space requirements mentioned earlier (the space is usually marked off). Your backboard and display should already be self-supporting, but it is wise to bring tools such as a screwdriver, hammer, extension cord, stapler, glue, and tape in case your project needs minor repairs or modifications.

After your project is completely set up, a fair representative will check it to make sure everything complies with the fair rules and safety regulations. Make sure that you have everything displayed properly and have any necessary instructions available for the fair staff or judges (this is especially important if you have a project that involves the use of a computer or some other type of mechanically operated display).

Judging at the State and Regional Fair Level

At some fairs, judging takes place as soon as all the projects are set up. Students and parents are not allowed in the exhibit hall during this time. Generally, judges are assigned to separate divisions as teams. They begin by reviewing the projects in their category individually and then as a group, in which they exchange thoughts with team members and rank the projects.

At the Connecticut Science Fair, the judges usually rank the projects on preliminary judging day by separating them into groups: Third honors (lower 50%), second honors (upper 50%), and first honors/finalist (top 10–15%). The third honors projects are determined first. The second honors and finalists are determined from the remaining projects. Only those projects that are finalists continue to compete for places in the overall competition. These finalists are notified by fair officials and asked to be present for final judging on the following day.

State science fair finalists are asked to give several oral presentations for various judges. These judges may represent the fair itself, professional or academic organizations, or businesses that distribute specialized awards.

Most state and regional science fair judges score contestants on these six criteria:

> *Scientific thought/engineering goals.* This area measures whether a project shows evidence of applied scientific or engineering development through cause and effect, verification of laws, applied techniques for efficiency, or presentation of a new concept.

> *Creative ability.* This portion measures the ingenuity and originality in your approach to your topic.

> *Thoroughness.* This area measures the variety and depth of the literature used, experimental investigation, and all other aspects of your project.

At most state and regional fairs, contestants are asked to give several presentations for both fair judges and special award sponsors from different organizations and businesses.

By having the opportunity to be present with your project during judging, you will be able to explain in detail certain procedures and conclusions in your project.

Skill. This aspect grades you on how much scientific and engineering practice you employed in your project. The level of experimentation, preparation, and treatment play an important role here.

Clarity. The exhibit should be presented in a way that is easily understood. Judges measure whether you have created a careful, systematic layout of selected information with neat, legible type.

Dramatic value. Judges also grade you on whether your project is presented in a way that attracts attention through the use of graphics and layouts and that appears interesting to viewers.

Keep in mind that judging is a difficult task that requires the skill and expertise of a wide range of qualified professionals. The judges are analyzing the quality of work that has been done on a subject matter that involves probing, testing, and reasoning in a creative sense. They are not interested in plain library research, meaningless collections, or copied text material.

Presenting Your Project in an Interview

By having the opportunity to be present with your project during judging, you are placed in an enviable position. You will be able to explain in detail certain procedures and conclusions in your project. It is important to be concise and business-like during this process. Give a meaningful summary of your work in an interview. Practice what you want to say first, before the fair, so that your presentation will be smooth and relaxed.

If a judge asks you a question for which you do not have an answer, explain that you have not come across that aspect in your research but that you would be glad to

Finalists should be sharp and strive to communicate accurately and thoroughly with judges.

inform the judge about another stage or area about which you are more knowledgeable. Above all, do not make up a false explanation. The judge is obviously capable of detecting any errors or "fudged" experimental results. Also, remember that the judge might already have seen a project similar to yours at another science fair.

Judging usually takes a few hours, so try to be consistent with every interviewer. Try to stay alert and concentrate on what you want to say. If you must leave your project momentarily, leave a note stating that you will return soon. General tips you should keep in mind for successful presentation are: Know your material, be confident, communicate well, and be thorough.

Specialized Awards

At some science fairs, there are also special areas of competition that are separate from the general fair honors. These special categories are accessible to those students who complete a project concentrated in a particular area of science. Besides being eligible for a regular award, these students may receive awards in the areas of mathematics, computer science, or energy and environmental sciences. Other specialized awards are presented by various companies and organizations. These groups honor excellence in a subject area related to the particular field that their organization specializes in.

After final judging, scores are tallied and the winners in each division are announced. The top high school projects of an affiliated state or regional fair qualify for competition in the International Science and Engineering Fair. Simply making it to the state or regional fair level is an honor, but only a few can experience the prestige of participating in the ISEF.

International Science and Engineering Fair

The ISEF is the grand finale of all state and regional fairs in the United States and several other countries. The top high school students in each ISEF-affiliated fair can compete at this fair, which is held annually in a major city, usually in the United States. The fair has an average of about 1,000 contestants, who account for more than 400 affiliated fairs. To see if there is a state or regional science fair near you, see Appendix C.

The procedures at the ISEF are slightly different than those of its affiliates. Students may select one of 16 categories in which to enter a project. Judging is essentially the same as in all the state and regional fairs, with the exception that it takes place on only one day. The contestants begin their day with interviews by a panel of judges. If they do well, they proceed into another round of judging. If they qualify again, they proceed to the third and final rounds, in which category winners are selected.

The ISEF is organized by Science Service, Inc., a national, nonprofit group. If you would like more information about the ISEF or affiliated science fairs in your area, write to:

Science Service, Inc.
1719 N St., N.W.
Washington, D.C. 20036

Closing Notes

This book was written to alleviate the frustration that often arises when students begin their first science project. It attempts to explain the strategies and shortcuts often used by finalists. Although the book cannot guarantee that you will make it to the top with your first science project, it can improve your chances and increase your motivation for future successes with science projects. Chances are good that your achievement will be recognized by college and business recruiters, who are looking for scientific talent and dedication. Remember, many of today's respected scientists began their careers in research and engineering by participating in science fairs. You can do so as well by investing your time and talent in a science fair project.

Summary

1. It is important that contestants check with state science fair officials to register on time and in the correct category and division.

36

2. Most state and regional fair judges score contestants on these six criteria:
   a. Scientific thought/engineering goals
   b. Creative ability
   c. Thoroughness
   d. Skill
   e. Clarity
   f. Dramatic value
3. Finalists should be concise and businesslike during the judging process and should strive to communicate with honesty and thoroughness.

7

COMPLETING AN AWARD-WINNING RESEARCH PROJECT

The purpose of this chapter is to take an in-depth look at the research and experimental techniques of a veteran science fair contestant. Unlike the 50 sample project outlines provided in this book, this section will examine an award-winning high school project from the origination of an idea through four years of research.

A Four-Year Microbiological Study of Carpets

Germination of an Idea

After Christopher Waluk came home from school with strep throat during the winter of 1991, it was not long before his younger brothers contacted the infectious bacteria from him. Two weeks later, just as Christopher appeared to have gotten over strep throat, he started to develop a sore throat all over again. In fact, this cycle repeated itself throughout the rest of the Waluk household as family members seemed to pass the insidious bacteria back and forth. During this time, Christopher's mother sterilized everything in sight in an effort to stop one family member from transferring the bacteria to another; everything, that is, except the living room carpet.

The family eventually recovered from their bout with strep throat, but Christopher wondered if the living room carpet in his home had anything to do with spreading the bacteria. Since he and his brothers tracked through the carpet every day, carried food into the living room, and spent many hours sitting or lying on the carpet to read or watch television, Christopher wondered if the carpet created an ideal breeding ground for microbes buried deep within its fibers. At this point, Christopher found himself at the beginning of an intriguing scientific investigation that would spark four award-winning science fair projects on different phases of this idea.

Phase I: Designing the Initial Research Plan and Experiment

Before doing anything else, Christopher scheduled an appointment with his science advisor, Sister Mary Christine, to discuss the specific direction in which to take his project idea and the type of scientific research that would be required to carry out his goals. Although Christopher was in the eighth grade and did not have any formal exposure to microbiology in the classroom setting, he did have an introductory knowledge of some microbiological lab techniques from attending the Science in Summer program conducted by Dr. Arthur Repak at the University of New Haven in West Haven, Connecticut.

Christopher's goal with the first phase of this project was to examine various types of carpeting from wool to plush nylon, in an effort to determine which one would retain the most bacteria after being washed with soap and water. Additionally, since many consumers treat their carpets with Scotchgard brand fabric protector, Christopher thought it might be interesting to expand his testing to see whether this substance would have any influence in inhibiting or encouraging the growth of bacteria.

He began his experiment by obtaining eight samples each of eight new carpets (each of a different composition) from a nearby carpet retailer and sterilizing them in boiling water. He sprayed half of the carpet samples from each carpet type with Scotchgard fabric protector and left the remaining four samples of each carpet type untreated. He then streaked *Serratia marcescens,* a common household bacteria obtained from a biological supply house, on one of the untreated samples made of 100 percent wool, as well as on the counterpart sample treated with the Scotchgard. He repeated this procedure with three other common household bacteria strains also obtained from a biological supply house, namely: *Streptococcus lactis, Streptomyces antibioticus,* and *Escherichia coli,* which were separately applied to the three remaining pairs of samples of the 100 percent wool carpet. He then repeated this procedure and applied the four bacteria strains to the eight samples of each of the seven remaining carpet types. Christopher let all of these carpet samples stand for 12 hours.

At the end of the 12-hour period, Christopher washed all the samples with soap and water and allowed them to dry. In order to determine whether the bacteria remained in the carpets after being washed, he ran sterile applicators through each sample and streaked them separately onto marked petri dishes. The results were rather interesting. Of the 64 carpet samples studied, 53 tested positive for bacterial growth after being cleaned. Further, 6 of the carpets treated with Scotchgard had heavier bacterial growth than their untreated counterparts. Christopher's work earned him finalist honors at the 1991 Connecticut State Science Fair where his project attracted a great deal of attention. Because of the positive feedback he received from the judges at the state fair and his desire to further explore his topic, Christopher continued his investigation as a high school freshman.

Phase II: Expanding the Initial Investigation

Christopher Waluk designed the second phase of his science project to determine how long bacteria would stay viable in a carpet and what substances could be used to arrest their growth. He began his research by obtaining five samples each of 12 different carpet types from a carpet retailer, and sterilized them in boiling water. This time, along with the original four bacteria strains that were

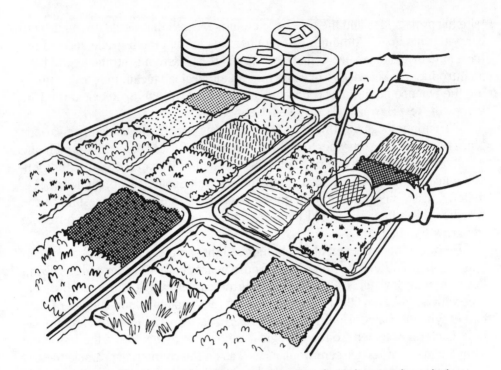

In the first phase of his investigation, Christopher ran sterile applicators through the carpet samples after they had been washed and streaked them separately onto marked petri dishes, in order to determine whether the bacteria remained present.

used in the last experiment, *Pseudomonas aeruginosa* was also transferred to the carpet samples. Every third day, Christopher took cultures of all the samples to determine how long the bacteria remained viable in each of the different carpet types. He continued this process for a full month and noted that the bacteria were still thriving in all of the carpet samples except two.

After realizing that most of the bacteria would probably remain viable for some time, Christopher decided to test typical store-brand carpet-cleaning products made specifically for shampooing and deodorizing carpets, along with a common household cleaning solution of white vinegar and water, to determine the effects each one might have on the existing carpet bacteria. To do so, Christopher passed several sterile applicators across each of the carpet samples and streaked them onto separately marked petri dishes. He then soaked sterile filter paper disks in each of the cleaning solutions and placed them individually onto the streaked petri dishes. All of the dishes were incubated for a period of 48 hours, and the effects of the store-brand cleaning solutions were analyzed. The results were startling and showed that none of the carpet shampooing and deodorizing products inhibited the growth of bacteria in any of the carpet samples tested. However, Christopher was surprised to note that the white vinegar and water solution did arrest most of the bacterial growth in the carpet samples.

At this point, Christopher decided to stop working with the carpet samples that were artificially impregnated with bacteria and take cultures directly from carpets in a multitude of homes in his town to determine if microbes other than

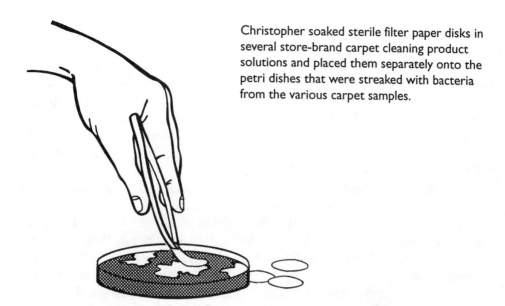

Christopher soaked sterile filter paper disks in several store-brand carpet cleaning product solutions and placed them separately onto the petri dishes that were streaked with bacteria from the various carpet samples.

the bacteria used in his initial studies were present. Christopher took cultures from a variety of carpet types and incubated them for 48 hours. Under the guidance of a local hospital lab technician, API tests and Catalase tests were performed on the cultures to identify the types of bacteria present. Much to Christopher's surprise, not only were all five of the bacteria strains originally studied found to be in the carpet samples, but, also, positive identification was made for pathogenic *Pseudomonas maltophilia, Klebsiella pneumoniae,* and *Staphylococcus aureus.*

At the 1992 Connecticut Science Fair, Christopher's work earned him a spot as a Connecticut Science Fair finalist once again, along with the opportunity to present his project and to network with scientific professionals in the field of microbiology, which proved to be the best reward of all. As it turned out, one of these professionals, Dr. Jon Geiger, was a scientist from the Connecticut-based Olin Research Center and had performed a great deal of research concerning the health effects of chemical emissions from carpets. He was greatly absorbed by the subject matter of Christopher's project, which apparently was not known to have been studied or discussed in the carpet industry, and spoke with Christopher at length concerning the importance of furthering the project. As a result, Christopher was invited to visit the Olin Research Center where he learned to conduct many advanced laboratory techniques which aided him in furthering his investigation into the microbial environment of carpets.

Phase III: Using Advanced Laboratory Techniques in the Investigation

During the summer after his first year in high school, Christopher met with Dr. Geiger at the Olin Research Center where he observed many advanced microbiological tests being conducted. At this point in his investigation, he decided to apply his new lab skills to a phenomenon that developed during the second phase of his project.

While observing those cultures taken directly from the carpets of various homes in his town, he noticed that there were several varieties of bacteria present at the same time in any given sample. Over time, Christopher noticed that one particular strain of bacteria seemed to overcome the other bacteria strains found to be present. He hypothesized that in an environment where different types of bacteria are present, there must be continuous competition among the bacteria strains for survival.

Christopher decided that the purpose of the third phase of his project would be to test more thoroughly to determine which carpet bacteria strain identified in Phase II of the project dominated the others and in which carpet types. To begin this portion of his project, he obtained several pieces of new carpeting from the carpet retailer as well as several pieces of new floor tile and oak wood flooring to serve as controls. He sterilized and inoculated each sample with the bacteria in various sequences and combinations utilizing the techniques he learned at the Olin Research Center. Christopher's results showed that *Pseudomonas aeruginosa* eliminated *Escherichia coli* in 14 carpets and was still viable at the end of a 40-day period. However, he found that in one carpet type they coexisted while there was no growth in two others. Other test results showed that *P. aeruginosa* eliminated *Serratia marcescens* in 11 carpets and was still viable at the end of a 40-day period as well. Still, in two carpet types the bacteria coexisted, and no growth occurred in four carpets. And, even though *S. marcescens* eliminated *E. coli* in 9 carpets and was still viable after a 40-day period, *P. aeruginosa* eliminated both *S. marcescens* and *E. coli* in 13 carpets and continued to remain viable after the 40-day period. Overwhelmingly, the *P. aeruginosa* overcame all carpet bacteria found to be present.

At the 1993 Connecticut Science Fair, Christopher placed fourth in the Senior Biological Division, and he received numerous awards and honors from various organizations including the United States Army. Christopher also received first place in the poster session of the Connecticut Junior Science and Humanities Symposium. Yet, despite the achievements he had made already, there was still more that Christopher wanted to know about the nature of the carpet microbes he had studied, and thus, the fourth and final phase of his investigation took form.

Phase IV: More Advanced Laboratory Techniques to Further the Investigation

During one of his visits to the Olin Research Center, Christopher had learned about biofilms, which are biological growths of microbial cells and extracellular polymers on a substratum that develop over a bacterium with time. In Phase IV of the project, Christopher's goal was to determine whether biofilms can establish themselves in carpet fibers, and if so, which types of carpet fibers are best suited for biofilms. Additionally, Christopher wanted to compare the different carpet bacterial combinations in the formation of biofilms and to determine whether any carpets with natural fibers have their own natural biocide that would inhibit or reduce the formation of a biofilm.

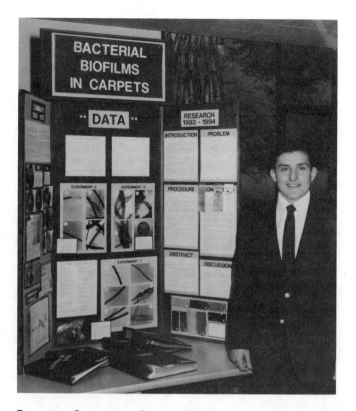

Four-time Connecticut Science Fair finalist, award winner, and
National Science and Humanities Symposium finalist
Christopher Waluk and his project.

Christopher began Phase IV by obtaining cultures from nine different household carpets. The bacteria samples were subcultured onto petri dishes and incubated for 48 hours. Gram stain tests were performed along with API and Catalase tests to identify the bacteria strains present, which included: *Klebsiella pneumoniae, Pseudomonas maltophilia, Escherichia coli, Pseudomonas aeruginosa, Staphylococcus,* and *Streptococcus.* Since Phase III showed that *Pseudomonas* eventually overcame all the bacteria strains present, Christopher decided to isolate the *P. aeruginosa* for the biofilm experiment. He then obtained various carpet type samples with both man-made and natural fibers and proceeded to carry out a series of complex tests to see if biofilms of the *P. aeruginosa* would form on the various types of fibers. When the experiment was completed, Christopher found that biofilms were present on all of the man-made fibers tested. However, of the natural fiber carpets, he found that only natural undyed wool did not provide an environment for biofilm formation.

The final phase of this microbiological project earned Christopher third place in the Senior Biological Division as well as many awards and distinctions. At the time this book went to press, Christopher was awarded an all-expenses paid trip to attend the 1995 National Junior Science and Humanities Symposium in Huntsville, Alabama.

50 Award-Winning Science Fair Projects

Important Notes Before You Begin

The following pages contain outline samples for 50 award-winning science fair projects. The summaries and diagrams should help to advise you on how to prepare your project, particularly if you are a first-time science fair participant. These outlines are not intended to do the work for you but to provide you with a variety of useful models to follow. The results of these 50 projects have thus been eliminated, and lists of questions have been prepared instead, so that you may have a guide for drawing conclusions about the projects.

The summaries of five International Science and Engineering Fair projects are marked and included throughout in order to give you a sense of the caliber that is required for this highest level of competition. You will see that one of the ISEF projects appears again in a different form (see projects 37 and 38). This second experiment is included so you can see how successful science fair projects can be further researched and developed into even more successful projects.

As you read through these projects, you may require information about where to obtain some of the scientific equipment mentioned in the experiments. Refer to Appendix B for a list of scientific supply companies from which laboratory equipment and other supplies may be purchased in your area. Also, some experiments list metric units of measure that may be unfamiliar to you or may require conversion to conventional units of measure. Refer to the metric conversion table at the beginning of the book for information about converting measurements.

Finally, you should keep in mind that the project outlines come from a variety of scientific disciplines and require minimal to advanced levels of scientific skill. They were developed by actual students in grades 7 through 12 and do not come from a lab workbook. Thus, there is no guarantee that any of the experimental procedures for any project will work as the experiment may indicate. The outlines represent award-winning work on different grade levels. Therefore, while students with little scientific experience may find some of the projects difficult, they should find others particularly suitable. Where noted, the assistance of a research scientist is required or precautions must be taken, and special skills are needed for certain projects. Be sure to heed these notices. They are there for your safety and to let you know whether or not a particular project is for you. In addition, check with your science fair project advisor for further guidance and safety precautions before starting any project appearing in this book. Most importantly, exercise common sense and good judgment when conducting any science experiment.

BEHAVIORAL SCIENCE

Which Characteristic Is Most Influential in Attracting Bees to a Flower: Fragrance, Color, or Flavor?

Note: Protective clothing should be worn and caution exercised when approaching the beehive.

Purpose

To determine the fragrance, color, and flavor that are most attractive to bees. Then, to determine which of these three characteristics plays the most important role in attracting bees.

Materials Needed

- pencil
- ruler
- 6 poster boards
- 9 assorted types of flowers
- scissors
- food processor
- cheesecloth
- cup
- brush
- colored construction paper (9 different shades are necessary: white, red, orange, yellow, green, blue, violet, light pink, and hot pink)
- glue
- sugar, lemon juice, salt, and chokecherries (or a food with a similarly bitter taste)
- beehive
- protective clothing

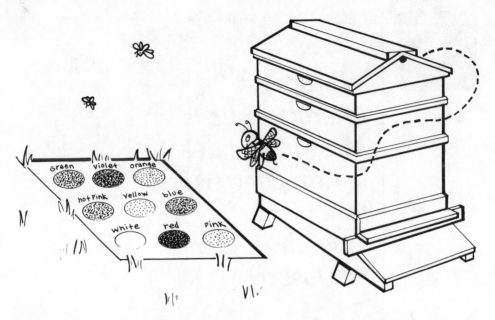

First, each poster board will be placed in front of the beehive to see which specific fragrance, color, and flavor are most attractive to the bees. Then, the three posters containing the separated variables only will be placed side by side to see which characteristic is most influential.

Experiment

The fragrance, color, and flavor variables will be isolated to identify the one that bees tend to go to first. For the fragrance test, several flowers that bees are known to pollinate will be pulverized individually in a food processor and strained through cheesecloth to collect the residue. The residue will then be streaked into separate circles on a poster board. For the color test, circles will be cut out of nine different shades of paper and glued onto another piece of poster board. For the flavor test, various flavors will be smeared over another poster board surface. Then, combinations of the three variables will be made. The bees' reactions and selections will be recorded.

Procedure

1. Draw nine 5-inch (12.7-cm) -diameter circles on one of the poster boards. Be sure to space them evenly on the board.

2. Obtain nine types of flowers and cut them from their stems. Pulverize them individually in a food processor. Then strain each pulverized flower through cheesecloth into the cup. With a brush, spread the residue from each flower in a separate circle on the poster board. Be sure to label the type of flower each smear came from.

3. Cut a 5-inch (12.7-cm) -diameter circle out of each sheet of construction paper. Space them randomly and evenly on another piece of poster board and glue them in place.

48

4. Take samples of the four basic food tastes (sweet, sour, salty, and bitter) from the sugar, lemon juice, salt, and chokecherries, and spread them separately on the third poster board. Be sure to label them.

5. For the remaining three poster boards, create the following combinations of characteristics: place each flower fragrance on a separate colored circle, place each flavor on a separate colored circle, and finally, mix the flavors with the various flower fragrances. Be sure to label them.

6. Begin your experiment with the first poster board of fragrances. Place the board approximately six feet (two meters) in front of the beehive and stand several feet further away. Note the fragrance to which the bees are consistently attracted. Remove the board and replace it with the board that contains only colors. Again, stand several feet away and see what color most attracts the bees. Do the same with the flavor board to see which flavor the bees are drawn to. Record your observations.

7. Verify your results by trying the combination boards. For example, if the bees in step 6 favored the color violet, a sweet flavor, and the fragrance of lilacs, see if those results hold true when the violet circle is covered with either the sugar or lilac residue.

8. Test to see which of the three characteristics is the most influential in attracting the bees by placing all three poster boards from step 6 side by side in front of the hive. Note the board that most consistently attracts the bees.

Results

1. Were all of the bees consistent in their preferences?
2. What fragrance, color, and flavor seemed to most attract the bees?
3. Did the bees tend to favor the same fragrance when it was combined with different colors and flavors? Did the same hold true for the color and flavor variables?
4. Which single characteristic appeared to be the most influential in attracting bees?

2

The Effects of Gender Identity on Short-Term Memory

Purpose

To graph and compare the effects of gender identity on the short-term memories of varying age groups of children.

Materials Needed

- 50 human subjects:
  5 boys and 5 girls in 1st grade
  5 boys and 5 girls in 2nd grade
  5 boys and 5 girls in 3rd grade
  5 boys and 5 girls in 4th grade
  5 boys and 5 girls in 5th grade

- grid containing 20 simple black and white pictures traditionally gender-typed for males (for example, a football) and for females (for example, a doll), arranged in alternate positions.
- stopwatch

Experiment

Each subject will be given 15 seconds to study the grid pictures. When the grid is taken away, the subject will be asked to list the names of the objects he or she can recall. It is believed that children will recall objects traditionally associated with their own gender.

Procedure

1. Test a child from each grade group individually in a quiet room that is free of distractions. Read the following directions to the participants: "I will show you some pictures for 15 seconds. When the time is up, I will take the pictures away and ask you to list the names of as many pictures as you can remember."

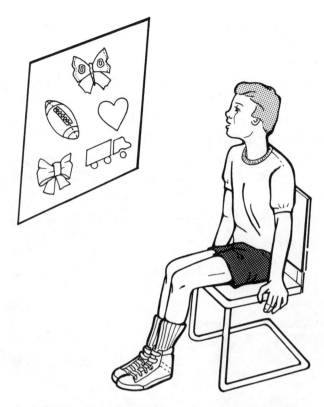

Each child will be given 15 seconds to study traditionally gender-typed grid pictures. When the grid is taken away, the subject will be asked to list the names of the objects he or she can recall.

2. Tabulate the results using two different methods of analysis.

First Analysis: Group your data according to whether each subject remembers a majority or a minority of the items traditionally associated with his or her gender or simply an equal number of both male- and female-gender-typed pictures.

Second Analysis: Examine whether there is a tendency for each age group, as well as the group as a whole, to be influenced by the gender-typing of the pictures presented. Record the total number and percentage of the male-gender-typed pictures recalled by the subjects as a group, and do the same with the female-gender-typed pictures. Do this for each grade level.

Results

1. Did the boys, as a whole group, recall a majority or a minority of male-gender-typed pictures? Or, did they recall an equal number of male- and female-gender-typed pictures?

2. Did the girls, as a whole group, recall a majority or a minority of female-gender-typed pictures? Or, did they recall an equal number of male- and female-gender-typed pictures?

3. When grouped by grade, did the boys recall male-gender-typed pictures at a greater frequency than female-gender-typed pictures?

4. When grouped by grade, did the girls recall female-gender-typed pictures at a greater frequency than male-gender-typed pictures?

5. Do the results change for each grade level? If so, what variables may have influenced the results of the varying grade levels? What are the implications of these results?

6. What do your results tell you about the group as a whole?

3

Do All Plants Transpire at the Same Rate Under Different Sources of Light?

Purpose

To determine if various species of plants transpire at the same rate under different sources of light.

Materials Needed

- 12 2-liter plastic soda bottles
- potting soil (enough to fill 12 soda bottle bottoms)
- scissors or cutting tool
- 3 young specimens each of 4 plant species (suggested: jade plant, African violet, ivy, polka dot plant)
- 3 cups (0.6 liter) water
- fluorescent lamp
- household lamp
- sunlight
- spatula
- graduated measuring cup

Experiment

Three plants of four different species will be placed in the removable bottoms of 12 plastic soda bottles. The removable tops of the soda bottles will be cut to fit within the soda bottle bottoms to form a kind of convertible terrarium. One sample of each plant species will be placed in the presence of all three different light sources: direct sunlight, a fluorescent lamp, and a household lamp, for a period of 6 hours. The amount of transpiration of the plants will then be compared and recorded.

Procedure

1. Pull the plastic supporting bottoms from the soda bottles and fill them with potting soil. Then cut the rounded bases from the upper portions of the soda bottles and put them aside.

2. Transplant the plants into the soda bottle bottoms.

3. Water each plant with ¼ cup (0.05 liter) of water and fit the soda bottle tops over the plants to create a terrarium (this will allow you to trap and measure the amount of water that the plants transpire). Be sure to place labels on each bottle top to specify the type of plant and the light source to which it will be exposed.

4. Place each plant species in the presence of all three light sources for 6 hours.

5. After the light exposure, remove the upper portions of the soda bottles carefully so that the water that has transpired onto them will not roll off. Then remove the water from each container with a spatula and measure with the measuring cup the quantity of water that transpired from each plant.

6. Repeat Steps 4 and 5 several times to obtain more accurate results.

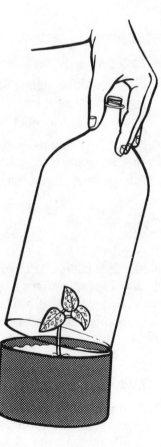

The plastic supporting bottoms will be removed from 2-liter soda bottles and used as pots for the various plants. Then, the rounded bases of the upper portions of the soda bottles will be cut to fit over the plants to form a terrarium.

Results

1. What amounts of water did each plant transpire under the different light sources?

2. Did the same plant species transpire equal amounts of water under all three light sources?

3. Which light source induced the most transpiration?

4. What outside variables may have influenced your results?

4

Can Plant Cloning Be Used Effectively by Produce Growers?

Purpose

To try to make a more perfect carrot and green bean by cloning rather than using the traditional cultivating methods, which may yield a lesser-quality vegetable or one that contains artificial chemicals and sprays. Also, to determine whether cloning is a faster and more effective means for farmers to grow crops.

Materials Needed

- carrot seeds from an unblemished organically grown carrot
- green bean seeds (same as above)
- pots for plants
- vermiculite
- greenhouse incubator
- seed germination medium
- glass beaker
- bunsen burner
- 30 petri dishes
- potting soil
- scalpel and forceps
- 5 fluid ounces (150 ml) callus initiation medium
- plastic bags
- 5 fluid ounces (150 ml) clone induction medium

Experiment

Some of the carrot and green bean seeds will be planted in vermiculite (to serve as a control of a traditional cultivating method) and some in the seed germination medium that has been melted into some of the petri dishes. After this latter group has grown, they will be transferred to the callus initiation medium then to the clone induction medium. The growth rates of the plants and the quality of their produce will be analyzed in comparison to the control plants and produce.

Procedure

1. Plant some of the carrot and green bean seeds in pots of vermiculite and put them into the greenhouse incubator. These will serve as the control group.

2. Melt the seed germination medium in the glass beaker over the bunsen burner and pour it into ten petri dishes equally. When solid, drop some of the carrot and green bean seeds onto the surface of the petri dishes. Growth will show in two weeks. These will serve as the experimental group.

3. When the plants in the control group are at least 4 inches (11.5 cm) tall, up-root them and put them into pots of potting soil. When the experimental plants are also 4 inches (11.5 cm) tall, cut their roots and leaves off with the scalpel. Cut their remaining stems into ½-inch (1-cm) pieces. Melt the callus initiation medium in the beaker over the bunsen burner and pour equally into ten other petri dishes. Next, place the stem sections onto the solidified petri dishes. Cover the dishes and put them into plastic bags.

4. Within a month, shoots will be visible. At this time, melt the clone induction medium and pour it into the remaining ten petri dishes. Using the scalpel, cut around the stem sections, including the callus initiation medium. With forceps, place the cuttings on the solidified clone induction medium. Cover the dishes and place them in the plastic bags.

5. As soon as growth is detected on the petri dishes, add some soil to the dishes to help the growth along. After these plants have grown a few inches, plant each of them into pots. Continue to care for the plants and observe their overall health and growth and the quality of their produce.

Results

1. Compare the growth of the seeds that were cultivated in the vermiculite and greenhouse incubator with those cultivated on the seed germination medium. Which plants grew faster? Which seeds look healthier?

2. Did the carrot plant or the green bean plant grow faster when it was cut and placed on the callus initiation medium?

3. Did the final plant clones look healthy? Did the difference in their original growth area affect their outcome?

4. Were the vegetables that were produced from the cloned plants as unblemished as their ancestors? Were they of higher quality than those produced from the control (vermiculite) plants?

5

How Effective Is Beta Carotene in Fighting Cancer in Plants?

Purpose

To determine whether beta carotene has any substantial effect in reducing or eliminating the presence of *Agrobacterium tumefaciens* in plants.

Materials Needed

- sunflower seeds
- beta carotene (vitamin A) solution (5 caplets to 1 pint (0.5 liter) water)
- tap water
- flower pots
- potting soil

- disinfectant
- inoculating needle
- candle or match
- *Agrobacterium tumefaciens* (a plant carcinogen)

Experiment

The sunflower seeds will be divided into three equal groups. Group A will be germinated in the beta carotene solution, while Groups B and C will be germinated in tap water only. After the seeds have germinated, they will be planted in potting soil. Groups A and B will be given the carcinogen and will serve as the experimental groups, while Group C will be carcinogen-free and serve as the control. Group A will then be watered twice a week with the beta carotene solution. Groups B and C will be watered twice a week with tap water. The growth of the plants will be monitored over a two-month period.

Procedure

Divide the sunflower seeds into three groups. Germinate the seeds in Group A in the beta carotene solution and the seeds in Groups B and C in tap water. After the

Draw some *Agrobacterium tumefaciens* onto the inoculating needle.

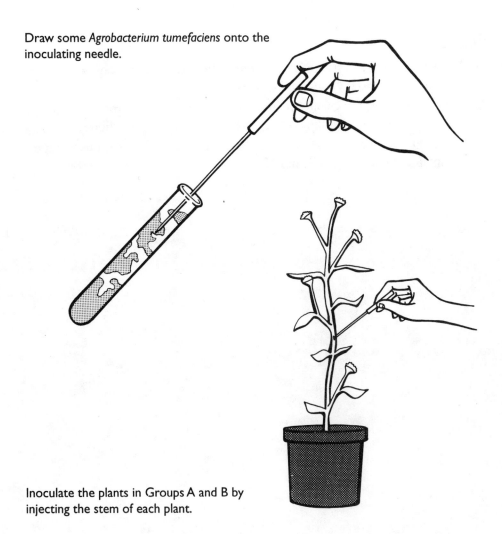

Inoculate the plants in Groups A and B by injecting the stem of each plant.

seeds have germinated, plant them in the flower pots in potting soil. Allow the plants to grow to approximately 7 to 10 inches (18 to 25 cm), after which the plants in Groups A and B will be ready for inoculation.

1. Thoroughly clean the working area with disinfectant.
2. Sterilize the inoculating needle by holding it for 3 seconds in the flame of the candle. Draw some of the *Agrobacterium tumefaciens* culture onto the needle tip and inject the plants from Group A. Then, sterilize the needle once again and inoculate the plants from Group B. Do not inoculate the plants from Group C, because it is the control group.
3. Continue to water the plants in Group A twice each week with the beta carotene solution and the plants in Groups B and C with tap water.
4. Record growth rates of the plants each week and note their appearance and rate of deterioration.

Results

1. Compare the growth of the plants before the inoculation process. Rate the plants according to their amount of growth and general condition.
2. Compare the growth of the plants after the inoculation process. Rate the plants according to their amount of growth and general condition.
3. Do you believe that the beta carotene solution had any effect in reducing or eliminating the disease in Group A?

The Effect of Electromagnetic Fields on Eremosphaera Algae Cells

Purpose

To determine if and how electromagnetic fields affect the number and appearance of algae cells at increasingly higher levels.

Materials Needed

- *Eremosphaera* algae colony
- 7 test tubes
- dropper
- slides
- microscope
- graduated measuring cup
- spring water
- masking tape
- marking pen
- electrical wire
- 2-light bathroom bar light fixture
- 2 Gro-Light brand fluorescent bulbs
- wood panel (upright and self-supporting)
- hammer and nails
- wall outlet
- thermometer

Experiment

The algae colony will be divided into seven equal groups and placed into seven test tubes filled with water. Groups 1 through 6 will be placed in an electromagnetic field by being encircled by increasing levels of spiraled electrical wire. Group 7 will serve as the control and will not be exposed to the electromagnetic field of the apparatus, by being placed in another room. The algae will be left within their electromagnetic fields for a period of time and will then be analyzed.

Procedure

1. Divide the *Eremosphaera* algae colony into seven equal groups in test tubes. Observe a droplet specimen from each group on a slide under a microscope. Record the appearance of the cell structures and the amount of cells present in each droplet. Fill each tube with ⅛ cup (30 ml) of spring water. Label the test tubes 1 through 7.

2. Wrap one layer of five coils of electrical wire (connected to a live circuit) around test tube 1, three layers of five coils around test tube 2 (= 15 spirals), six layers of five coils around test tube 3 (= 30 spirals), nine layers of five coils around test tube 4 (= 45 spirals), twelve layers of five coils around test tube 5 (= 60 spirals), and fifteen layers of five coils around test tube 6 (= 75 spirals) (see diagram). Test tube 7 will not be wrapped with electrical wiring.

3. Affix the test tubes below the light fixture equipped with the Gro-Light bulbs, allowing for a 6-inch (15-cm) space between each test tube (with the exception of tube 7 which will be exposed to the normal electromagnetic fields found in another room of your house).

4. Carefully nail the back of the light fixture to the wood panel. Then plug the apparatus into a nearby wall outlet.

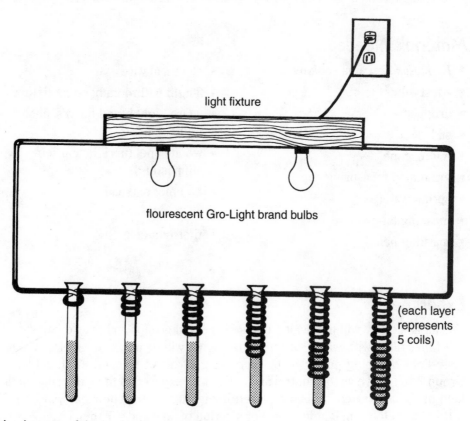

A schematic of the testing apparatus set-up.

5. Leave the tubes exposed for about an hour, then turn off the power and measure the temperature within each vial. Then, take a droplet specimen from each tube again to record your observations of the cell structures and the number of cells within each droplet. Repeat the experiment by exposing the test tubes to the electromagnetic fields for two additional hours and record your observations.

Results

1. Compare the appearance and number of cells found initially in each test tube to those found at the end of the experiment. Did they vary within the same tube?

2. Did cell appearance and quantity change from tube to tube? Were these changes more apparent as higher electromagnetic fields were introduced?

3. Compare the temperatures of all the tubes. At higher temperatures what changes occurred?

7

What Is the Most Efficient Substance for Melting Ice?

Purpose

To determine the most effective of seven substances traditionally used for melting ice.

Materials Needed

- 14 aluminum foil baking pans (8 × 8 × 2 inches) (20 × 20 × 5 cm)
- tap water to fill each pan
- masking tape
- marking pen
- 1 cup (0.24 liter) calcium chloride
- 1 cup (0.24 liter) of a commercial brand of melting crystals
- 1 cup (0.24 liter) sodium chloride
- 1 cup (0.24 liter) cat box litter
- 1 cup (0.24 liter) sand
- 1 cup (0.24 liter) rubbing alcohol
- 1 cup (0.24 liter) mineral rock salt
- large freezer (experiment can be done outside if temperature is below 32° F or 0° C)

Experiment

Fourteen aluminum foil baking pans containing ice will be subjected to equivalent amounts of different substances commonly used to melt ice. Each pan will be timed individually so as to determine which substance, and the way it is applied, is the most effective in melting the ice. Comparisons will then be made between each substance to see the amount of residue each has left and whether that residue could have damaging effects on paved driveways and sidewalks.

Procedure

1. Fill seven of the baking pans with water and freeze them either in a large freezer or outdoors. Label this lot Group A.

2. Pour one-half of each of the seven substances separately into the remaining seven baking pans. Label each pan with the name of its substance. Carefully fill the pans with water and place them in the freezer or outdoors to freeze. Label this lot Group B.

3. When the water in Group A has completely solidified, pour the remaining half of each substance into the separate pans. Label each pan with the name of its substance and return them to the freezer.

4. At this point, all 14 pans of water/ice will be in contact with one of the substances. Measure the amount of melting of each pan in Group A in half-hour intervals over a 3-hour period and record your results. Check on Group B in half-hour intervals also, noting the rate of ice formation, if any, over a 3-hour period. Record your results.

5. Pour some of the contents of each baking pan in Group A onto separate sections of a uniformly paved driveway and label. Pour some of the contents of the Group B pans into separate sections of a uniform cement sidewalk and label. Allow all of the water to evaporate. Let the different types of residue stay where they are for 4 to 6 weeks. After this time, sweep them away and note any damage that has resulted. Compare the effects of the same substances on both surfaces.

Results

1. Which substance in Group A melted the ice fastest? How well did this substance prevent the formation of ice in Group B?

2. Did the addition of the ice-melting substances prior to the application of water in Group B slow or prevent the formation of ice? Does this mean that such substances should be applied to driveways and sidewalks when precipitation and freezing temperatures are expected?

3. Did any of the substances' residues cause damage to either the paved driveway or the sidewalk? If so, what type of damage did you observe?

4. In terms of speed, efficiency, and cost, which substance was the best?

8

What pH Level Is Most Conducive to Corrosion in Iron and Copper?

Purpose

To determine the pH level that induces the most corrosion in the least amount of time in iron and copper in the presence of oxygen.

Materials Needed

- 14 glass cups
- hydrochloric acid
- sodium hydroxide
- distilled water
- litmus paper
- 28 test tubes
- iron filings to fill 14 test tubes halfway

- copper filings to fill 14 test tubes halfway
- masking tape
- marking pen
- a narrow plastic scooping tool
- paper towels

Experiment

Fourteen test tubes will be half filled with iron filings and another fourteen will be half filled with copper filings. Each tube will then receive a different solution of hydrochloric acid, sodium hydroxide, and distilled water of varying pH levels. The tubes will be exposed to the various solutions for one month, with the exception that they will be exposed to oxygen daily for 30 minutes. Each sample will be analyzed daily and at the end of the experiment to note its rate of corrosion.

Procedure

1. Fill 14 cups with varying proportions of the hydrochloric acid, sodium hydroxide, and distilled water to achieve pH levels from 1 (acidic) to 14 (alkaline). Test with litmus paper to make sure you have 14 different pHs. (In an acid solution, the paper will turn bright red. In an alkaline solution, the paper will turn blue.)

2. Fill 14 test tubes halfway with the iron filings and label the tubes from 1a to 14a. Fill the other 14 test tubes halfway with the copper filings and label them from 1b to 14b.

3. Pour some of each pH solution separately into the iron filing tubes and some separately into the copper filing tubes. Each test tube should be about three-fourths full.

4. Leave the filings inside their respective pH solutions for about 30 days, but allow the filings to air out by scooping them out of their test tubes and laying them on separate paper towels for 30 minutes each day. Observe and record the changes that take place in each test tube daily.

Results

1. Which pH level induced the most corrosion in the iron filings? In the copper filings? Which pH level induced the fastest rate of corrosion on iron? On copper? How soon after the beginning of the experiment did you observe these changes?

2. Did the higher pH levels induce more corrosion than the lower pH levels?

3. Did the iron and the copper corrode in the same way?

4. Did any of the pH levels appear to inhibit corrosion?

9

How Effective Is Lobster Shell Chitin in Filtering Wastewater Metallic Ions?

Purpose

To test the filtration abilities of chitin; to compare it with charcoal, a common water filter; and to determine how chitin absorbs metals.

Materials Needed

- 6 test beakers
- metals (iron, lead, zinc, iridium, tin, and silver) and solvents for preparing 6 different (100 mg/L metal solutions)
- distilled water
- Standard Methods of Atomic Absorption (can be found in a chemistry book)
- 12 5-inch (12-cm) squares of cheesecloth
- glass tube (open at both ends)
- 6 rubber bands

- 12 ounces (300 g) chitin (obtained by cleaning, drying, and chopping lobster shells into ¼-inch (0.5-cm) pieces) per metal solution
- ringstand and clamps
- funnel
- Atomic Absorption Instrument to measure a solution's metallic concentration
- stopwatch
- glass cup
- 12 ounces (300 g) activated carbon (charcoal) per metal solution

Experiment

Several solutions of metals and solvents will be filtered through chitin and charcoal. The filtration effectiveness of each will be compared by measuring the amount of time it takes for each solution to run through both filters and by measuring the concentration of metallic ions present in the solutions' effluent after they have passed through both filters.

Procedure

1. In six separate beakers, prepare a 100 mg/L solution for each of the types of metals, according to the Standard Methods of Atomic Absorption.

2. Fold one square of cheesecloth into four layers and secure it over one end of the glass tube with a rubber band. Place 2 ounces (50 g) of the chitin into the other end of the tube. Then, attach the tube to the ringstand and place the funnel on the glass tube.

3. Remove 2 teaspoons (10 ml) of one solution, measure its metallic concentration with the Atomic Absorption Instrument, and record it. This will be the control. Pour the remaining solution through the apparatus and use the stop-

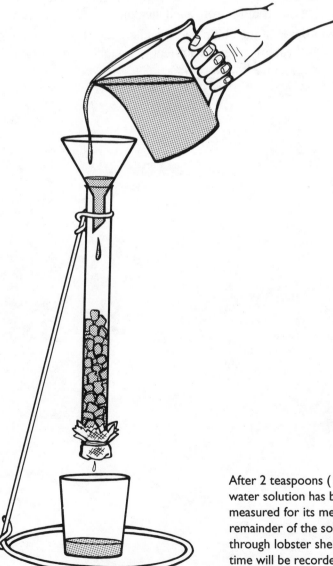

After 2 teaspoons (10 ml) of the metallic/water solution has been removed and measured for its metallic concentration, the remainder of the solution will be poured through lobster shell chitin, and its filtering time will be recorded along with the effluent's metallic concentration.

watch to record the time it takes for the solution to run through the filter and collect as effluent into the cup. Then, test the effluent's metallic concentration with the Atomic Absorption Instrument and record it.

4. Repeat steps 2 and 3 with the other metallic solutions. Whenever a different solution is used, clean the tube and use new chitin, cheesecloth and rubber bands.

5. Then, repeat steps 1 through 4, replacing the chitin with 2 ounces (50 g) of charcoal for each metallic solution.

Results

1. Compare the concentrations of the solutions before and after filtration. What percentage of metal did the chitin remove from each solution? What percentage of metal did the charcoal remove from each solution?

2. Compare the filtration times of the chitin and the charcoal. Does the rate at which a solution passes through either filter affect its metallic concentration?

3. Which metals were absorbed best in the chitin?

10

How Does Saltwater Mix in an Estuary?

Purpose

To determine the average and individual concentrations of salt found in water from various points along an estuary by analyzing the color, density, and residue of the water.

Materials Needed

- 2-quart (-liter) samples of estuary water from seven locations along an estuary
- 250-ml beaker
- 14 test tubes
- 4-quart (-liter) sample of fresh river water (or substitute distilled water)
- 4-quart (-liter) sample of saltwater
- metric graduated cylinder
- 15 plastic cups
- balance scale

Experiment

Three different tests will be used to analyze estuary water. The first test will focus on color variations to distinguish the saltwater from the river water. The second will measure the density of the estuary water to determine the amount of saltwater from the sea that has been mixed in. The third test will measure the residual percentage of salt after the water has evaporated.

Procedure

Test A—To determine visually the average amount of saltwater present within samples from various locations along an estuary.

1. Boil the seven 2-quart (-liter) samples of estuary water separately until each is reduced to 250 ml. Then fill seven test tubes halfway with each of the concentrated samples.

2. Next, make seven saltwater/fresh river water color reference samples in the other seven test tubes with which to compare the concentrated estuary samples. Fill the first test tube halfway with 100% fresh river water, the second with 80% fresh river water and 20% saltwater, the third with 60% fresh river water and 40% saltwater, the fourth with 50% fresh river water and 50% saltwater, the fifth with 40% fresh river water and 60% saltwater, the sixth with 20% fresh river water and 80% saltwater, and the seventh with 100% saltwater (see diagram).

3. Compare the colors of the samples of concentrated estuary water with the colors of the reference samples. For each estuary sample, record the reference sample that most closely resembles it in color.

Test B—To determine the actual amount of saltwater
mixed in by calculating the densities of the seven samples.

1. Using the graduated cylinder, measure 175 cc of each estuary sample into a plastic cup and weigh each cup separately on the balance scale. Then subtract the cup's weight to obtain the mass of each sample.

2. Find the density of each sample by dividing the mass by the volume. Then calculate the average density for all the samples.

3. Next, find the actual percentage of saltwater for each sample. Once you have determined the separate and combined densities of the fresh water and saltwater in your sample and know the sample's total volume, the percentage of fresh river water (x) and saltwater (y) can be calculated as follows:

[(volume of x) (density of x)] + [(volume of y) (density of y)] = total volume $\times$ density

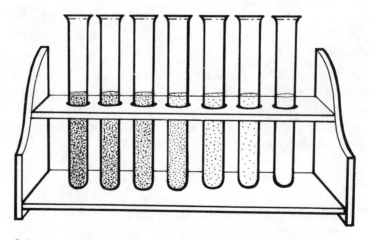

Saltwater and fresh river water color reference samples should be made with which to compare the concentrated estuary samples. Fresh river water is usually several shades browner than mixed fresh river water and saltwater, while saltwater is usually clear.

Test C—To measure the residual percentage of salt in each sample.

1. Pour the remaining estuary samples each into a separate plastic cup. Place another cup alongside and fill it with distilled water until its volume is the same as each of the sample cups.
2. Weigh the cup containing the distilled water on the balance scale and record its mass. Then, weigh both cups on the balance scale and subtract the mass of the distilled water from the mass of the sample water. Repeat for each of the samples and record your results.

Results

1. What were the levels of salt concentration among the samples? Were your color reference samples accurate as to the salt concentrations in each sample?
2. Were the results from each of the three tests consistent for each water sample?
3. Were the salinity levels consistent for all seven locations? If not, which location of the estuary had the highest level of salinity? The least?
4. Experiment with different estuaries. Are the salinity level distributions that you found in the original estuary comparable to those of other estuaries?

CHEMISTRY

Can the Life Span of a Soap Bubble Be Extended in Different Temperatures and Atmospheric Conditions?

Purpose

To determine if certain substances can increase the life span of soap bubbles under varying temperatures and atmospheric conditions.

Materials Needed

- 1 cup (240 ml) dishwashing liquid
- tap water
- 3-quart (-liter) glass, metal, or plastic container
- 9 plastic drinking straws
- stopwatch
- 8 clear glass jars with covers
- bubble additives:
  1 teaspoon (5 ml) school glue
  3 drops food coloring

- ¼ teaspoon (1 ml) vanilla extract
- ¼ teaspoon (1 ml) witch hazel
- ¼ teaspoon (1 ml) olive oil
- ¼ teaspoon (1 ml) aftershave lotion
- ¼ teaspoon (1 ml) lemon juice
- masking tape
- marking pen
- thermometer

Experiment

Bernoulli's principle of raising and lowering a bubble by changing the air pressure will be tested with bubbles made from liquid soap under two types of

74

atmospheric conditions: a hazy, hot, and humid environment and a clear, cold environment. The same principle will be tested again when the soap bubbles are mixed with bubble additives to see whether the bubbles will be altered in the same two environments. Finally, both types of bubbles will be blown into eight glass jars, covered, and placed in a warm room. The life span of each bubble will be timed until it pops. The same will be done in a cold room. Comparisons will be made between additives under differing temperatures and atmospheric conditions.

Procedure

1. On a hazy, hot, and humid day, mix a solution of ½ cup (120 ml) dishwashing liquid with 2 quarts (liters) water in the container outdoors. Dip one end of a straw into the solution and blow from the other end to create a bubble. Shake the straw lightly to detach the bubble. With a stopwatch, time the life span of the bubble while testing Bernoulli's principle (wave your hand over the

In step 3, after the bubble additives have been mixed into seven of the eight jars, blow a bubble directly inside each jar and time its life span to see which substance holds a bubble the longest in a warm and in a cold environment.

bubble to make it rise, then wave your hand under the bubble to make it sink). Repeat the same procedure on a clear, cold day. Note any changes in the way the bubble forms and the length of time it remains intact.

2. Mix another solution of ½ cup (120 ml) dishwashing liquid and 2 quarts (liters) of water. Pour equal amounts of the solution into the eight jars. Add the specified amount of a different bubble additive to each jar, stir until dissolved, and label each jar. The eighth jar is the control and will contain soap bubbles only. Then, repeat step 1 for the seven jars containing bubble additive and record your results.

3. Bring all eight of the jars indoors. Using a different straw for each mixture, blow a bubble directly into each of the jars. Cover the jars immediately and place them in a warm room heated to 80 degrees Fahrenheit. Observe each bubble and record the time it takes for each to pop. Repeat this step in a room cooled to 45 degrees Fahrenheit. You may also use a refrigerator.

Results

1. Did the air pressure within the plain soap bubbles change under different atmospheric conditions? If so, how did the bubbles react, and how long did they exist under each condition?

2. Did the bubble additives have any effect in changing the way the bubbles reacted to each environment? If so, what were these effects?

3. Did the plain soap bubbles or the bubbles with additives last longer under warmer or colder temperatures?

4. In which bubble additive solution did the bubbles last the longest under all conditions?

5. What practical applications might this experiment have for industry?

CHEMISTRY

What Colored Dyes Are Found in Powdered Drink Mix and Colored Marking Pens?

Purpose

To find out which colored dyes are used in powdered drink mix and in colored marking pens.

Materials Needed

- pencil
- ruler
- filter paper cut into twenty 6-by-6-inch (15-by-15-cm) squares
- 10 packages of powdered drink mix, each of a different variety
- tap water
- dropper
- 10 small plates
- stapler
- 20 glass jars with lids (or substitute plastic wrap)
- rubbing alcohol
- 10 differently colored marking pens
- timer

Experiment

Paper chromatography, which separates a mixture into its component pigments, will be used to analyze the various colored dyes present in ten flavors of drink mix and ten differently colored marking pens.

Procedure

1. Make pencil marks 3/4 inch (2 cm) up from the bottom on both lower corners of ten of the cut-out squares. Draw a line connecting the marks.

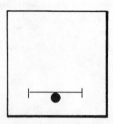

A 6-by-6-inch (15-by-15-cm) square, cut from the filter paper, with the drink mix or marking pen spot.

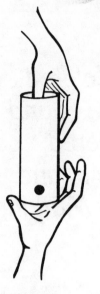

After the spot has dried, roll the filter paper into a cylinder and staple.

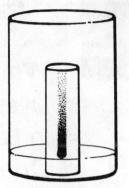

When the cylinder is placed in the center of the jar of rubbing alcohol for 15 to 20 minutes, the spot of drink mix or marking pen will separate into its component color

2. Mix a pinch of each variety of powdered drink mix with a drop of water on each of the ten small plates.

3. With the dropper place a droplet of a different variety beneath the pencil line of each filter and allow them to dry. Label the names of each flavor in pencil.

4. When each paper has dried, staple each into a cylinder shape, with the droplet stain on the outside.

5. Fill ten jars about ½ inch (1 cm) high with rubbing alcohol.

6. Place one paper cylinder into each jar without touching the sides of the jars.

7. Cover the jars with lids or plastic wrap.

8. Leave each paper cylinder in the alcohol for about 15 to 20 minutes or until the alcohol reaches the top of the paper.

9. Remove the paper filters and allow them to dry. You have just made a chromatogram and should be able to see the different colored dyes that make up each of the powdered drink mixes used.

10. To experiment with the colored marking pens, repeat steps 1 through 9, making colored marks on the paper filters instead of using the drink mix.

Results

1. Were there more pigments in the chromatograms of the drink mixes or the colored marking pens? What colors were visible in each chromatogram?

2. What pigments were found most often in the drink mixes? What pigments were found most often in the marking pens?

3. Were the lighter-colored drink mixes and marking pens made up of as many pigments as the darker ones?

4. Which of the component dyes traveled furthest up the filter paper? Why?

5. Were the drink mixes and marking pens of the same color made up of different pigments?

COMPUTER SCIENCE/MATHEMATICS

Can Mathematical Patterns Be Found in Johann Sebastian Bach's Two-Movement Preludes and Fugues?

Purpose

To determine whether there are any mathematical patterns in the composition of Johann Sebastian Bach's two-movement preludes and fugues.

Materials Needed

- computer with attached printer
- computer spreadsheet software for analyzing data and constructing graphs

- sheet music: *Johann Sebastian Bach, Complete Preludes and Fugues For Organ* by Dover Publications, Inc., 1985

Experiment

For each composition, the total number and frequency of notes, the number and frequency of notes in each line of music, and the number and frequency of notes in each measure will be analyzed, along with the ratios of the number of notes between the various lines of music.

Procedure

1. Count the number of notes in the treble, bass, and pedal lines of each measure in each musical composition. Access the data-analyzing computer software

program and enter this data. Use the software to calculate the total number of notes in each line of music and compose a graphical representation of your data. Print out your graph and visually inspect.

2. Count the number of measures in each musical composition and enter this data into your computer. Again, use the software to compose a graphical representation of your data and print for visual inspection.

3. Use the data entered into the computer to print out individual graphs of the number of notes in each of the treble, bass, and pedal lines of each measure for each work and check for patterns.

4. Use the computer data to calculate the ratio of the number of notes in the treble line of each measure to the number of notes in the bass line of each measure. Produce a graphical representation of these ratios and inspect for any patterns.

5. Use the computer data to calculate the total number of notes in each work and then take the square root of these numbers. Produce a graphical representation of this data and inspect for any patterns.

6. Use the data produced in step 1 and calculate how many times a number appeared as the total number of notes in a measure, for each musical composition. Produce a graphical representation of these results.

7. Compare all graphs for results.

Results

1. Was there a set ratio between the number of notes in any two lines of music? Does Bach use a certain number of notes in some measures more than others?

2. Did the number of measures in the minor key works vary more than the number of measures in the major key works?

3. Were you able to detect any mathematical patterns? Try to expand this experiment to determine if other mathematical patterning possibly exists.

14

Measuring the Brightness of an Incandescent Light Bulb

Note: Conduct this experiment under the supervision of an adult who is experienced in electrical wiring. Exercise caution when testing the light bulbs for prolonged periods of time. The International Science and Engineering Fair has established strict guidelines to which all of its affiliate fairs must adhere. These guidelines involve what is unacceptable for display and operation at an affiliated science fair. It is the responsibility of the student to follow these rules carefully. (See the Foreword and/or contact Science Service, the administrator of the ISEF, for a copy of the applicable rules.)

Purpose

To measure the amount of energy given off by various 60-watt incandescent light bulbs to determine if there are differences between the brightnesses of bulbs from different manufacturers.

Materials Needed

- Solar Project Set by Radio Shack, Part No. 277–1201 (comprised of a solar cell connected with wires to a DC motor)
- 7-inch (18-cm) wooden dowel
- 8-by-8-inch (20-by-20-cm) wooden board
- several 3½-inch nails
- 2 washers
- plastic lid from a coffee can
- mechanical revolution counter
- 9-by-9-inch wooden board
- 6-by-4-inch (15-by-10-cm) wooden board

- 12-by-24-inch (30-by-60-cm) wooden board
- electric wall switch
- electric lamp socket
- 2 electric outlet boxes
- electric cord with plug
- 15 unused incandescent light bulbs including 3 bulbs from 5 different companies (60 watt, 120VAC, (standard life)
- stopwatch
- an adult helper

Experiment

A number of 60-watt incandescent light bulbs from different manufacturers will be tested to determine if the brightness of the bulbs can be measured effectively by converting light energy into electrical energy. The energy produced by the bulbs will be converted by a solar cell into electrical energy which will be used to drive a motor that will turn a counter. Readings will be taken from the counter to record the amount of energy generated from each light bulb. The results for each manufacturer's bulb will be compared to determine if all 60-watt bulbs offer the same brightness of light.

Procedure

Construct the light bulb testing mechanism (see diagram)

1. Mount the DC motor from the Solar Project Set onto the end of the wooden dowel.
2. Fasten the dowel to the 8-by-8-inch board with the nail and two washers in a manner that will allow it to pivot. Mount the coffee can lid to the shaft of the mechanical revolution counter in a manner that will allow it to turn the numbers on the counter when moved by the shaft of the motor. Mount the apparatus to the 9-by-9-inch board.
3. On the 6-by-4-inch board, attach the solar panel, which is connected to the DC motor by wires, as shown in the diagram.
4. Assemble the light bulb testing mechanism by mounting both the 6-by-4-inch solar panel unit and the 9-by-9-inch DC motor apparatus to the 12-by-24-inch board, as shown in the diagram.

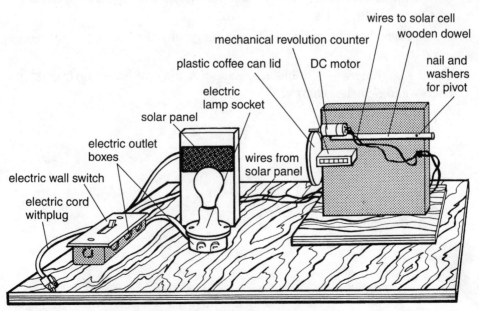

The light bulb testing mechanism ready for experimentation.

5. Complete the unit by mounting the electric wall switch (turns on the light bulb) as well as the electric lamp socket unit to their outlet boxes and onto the 12-by-24-inch wooden board, as shown in the diagram. Attach the electric cord with plug to the electric wall switch outlet box. Since there may not be enough light to drive the motor if the solar cell is too far away from the subject bulb, be sure that the solar cell is placed approximately 1 inch (2.5 cm) away from the bulb.

Test the light bulbs

1. With the light switch in the off position, fasten a light bulb from a particular manufacturer into the light socket.
2. Set the counter to zero and set the stopwatch for 60 seconds.
3. Turn on the light switch at the same time that you start the stopwatch.
4. At 60 seconds, turn off the switch and record the number on the counter.
5. Remove the light bulb from the socket and repeat steps 1 through 4 with the remaining light bulbs from the same manufacturer. Record your data and average your test results for this one manufacturer.
6. Repeat steps 1 through 5 for the bulbs from the other manufacturers. Be sure not to leave any light bulb on for more than three minutes at a time since the sensitive housing of the plastic solar cell could melt.

Results

1. Was there uniformity in counter readings between the sampled bulbs of the same manufacturer? If not, by what margin did the results vary?
2. If there are discrepancies between some of the same company bulb readings, why do you think this is so?
3. Which brand light bulb, if any, offered the greatest amount of brightness as evidenced by your data?
4. Can the brightness of light bulbs be measured effectively by converting light energy into electrical energy?

15

Which Form of Insulation Is Most Effective?

Purpose

To test the effectiveness of various forms of insulation and to determine which would effectively retain the most heat and serve as the best insulator for warming the human body.

Materials Needed

- equal portions of wool, flannel, human hair (can be obtained from a barbershop), thermal insulation, cotton, and chicken feathers (enough to pad both sides of the interior of a plastic bag 1-inch (2.5-cm) thick)
- 7 large plastic resealable bags
- masking tape

- 7 pints (3.5 liters) tap water
- 7 1-pint (0.5-liter) canning jars with lids
- oven thermometer
- 7 total immersion lab thermometers
- refrigerator

Experiment

Seven water-filled jars will serve as models of the human body. The plastic bags filled with insulating materials will represent the insulated clothing being tested.

Procedure

1. Insert one type of insulating material into each plastic bag. Fasten the insulating materials to the insides of the bags with masking tape to equal 1 inch (2.5 cm) thick all around. Leave the seventh bag empty to serve as a control.
2. Boil the water and fill each of the seven jars with equal amounts.
3. Immediately take the temperature of each jar with the oven thermometer and record your data. When the temperature reaches 98.6 degrees Fahrenheit (37

When the temperature reaches 98.6 degrees
Fahrenheit (37 degrees Celsius) in each jar, drop a
total immersion lab thermometer into each jar and cap
it quickly. Then, put each jar into a different insulator
pouch.

degrees Celsius) in each jar, drop a total immersion lab thermometer into
each jar, and cap it tightly and quickly.

4. Put each jar into a different insulator pouch (including the empty pouch) and
place in the refrigerator.

5. Keep the jars in the refrigerator for 2 hours. Take the temperature readings of
each jar every 15 minutes and cap quickly after each reading. (Some total
immersion lab thermometers have to have their mercury columns shaken
down for each new reading.) At the end of the 2 hours, compare readings and
note how rapidly they changed over time relative to one another.

Results

1. Was the jar in the control bag colder than the insulated jars?

2. Which insulating material was most effective?

3. Which insulating material was the easiest to work with and would be the most
practical in winter clothing? What other insulators could be used in this experiment?

16

Alcohol as a Fuel: Recycling Wastes into Energy

Note: A permit must be obtained from the Bureau of Alcohol, Tobacco, and Firearms before you begin this experiment.

Purpose

To see if it is possible for a household to construct a simple and inexpensive still capable of recycling its fermented organic garbage into a grade of ethyl alcohol that would meet most of the household's energy needs.

Materials Needed

- 6 feet (1.8 meters) of ⅓-inch (0.85-cm) copper tubing
- coffee can with top and bottom removed
- small bowl
- pressure cooker
- oven thermometer
- 2-gallon (7.6-liter) plastic container
- 1½ gallons (5.7 liters) warm sterile water
- 1 cup (0.24 liter) granulated sugar
- 3 cups (0.72 liter) pureed apple peelings

- sugar hydrometer
- 1 teaspoon (5 ml) active dried yeast
- fermentation lock
- cheesecloth
- proof hydrometer
- ice
- kitchen stove
- 4 fuel-burning lamps
- 16 ounces (0.45 kg) each gasoline, benzene, and kerosene
- adult helper

Experiment

A small portion of sugar and apple peelings will be used to simulate a fraction of a household's weekly organic garbage output. These items will then be combined with water and active dried yeast for distilling in a plastic container. This mixture will be allowed to ferment for approximately 4 to 5 days in a warm, dark environment. The fermented substance will then be placed in a simple pressure cooker still and will be distilled into alcohol. The amount of fuel produced will be measured and multiplied by the weekly output of organic garbage per household to determine the average amount of ethyl alcohol a household could produce. The alcohol will then be tested to compare its burning time and environmental effects with that of more traditional energy fuels.

Procedure

Part I—Build the still.

1. Apply for a permit from the local Bureau of Alcohol, Tobacco, and Firearms to produce a small portion of ethyl alcohol for home fuel experimentation.

2. Begin your experiment by constructing a simple pressure cooker still. With the help of an adult, coil half of the copper tubing five times (leaving the other half extended) and fit the coil within the coffee can so that the end of the coil bends down and out of the bottom of the can into a bowl. Bend the remaining extended copper tubing in an arc over to the pressure cooker. The end of the tubing should hook over the top of the stem on the cooker's lid.

3. Remove the pin from the lid of the pressure cooker and place the oven thermometer in its place. (This will measure the temperature of the alcohol within the pot.) Put the still aside.

Part II—Ferment the organic garbage.

1. Fill the plastic container with the warm sterile water. Add the sugar and the pureed apple peelings. This entire mixture, which is called *mash*, should consist of exactly 20 percent sugar from the table sugar (sucrose) and the sugar found naturally in the apple peelings (fructose). This percentage can be accurately determined by placing the sugar hydrometer into the mash.

2. Mix these items well and add the active dried yeast for distilling to the mash. Cover the container and place the fermentation lock in the lid of the container. The lock will indicate when fermentation has begun and when it has ended. Place the entire unit in a warm, dark environment at around 80 degrees Fahrenheit (27 degrees Celsius) (such as a furnace room) to ferment for about 4 to 5 days. If there are bubbles in the fermentation lock, then fermentation is occurring; if there are no bubbles in the lock, then fermentation has ceased.

Part III—Distill the fermented mash.

1. After fermentation, strain the mash through a cheesecloth, measure the amount of liquid yield, and measure its alcohol proof with the proof hydrometer. Then place the liquid into the pot of the pressure cooker and attach the lid with its copper coil system that you built in Part I. Fill the coffee can unit with ice. Place the still unit onto a stove and heat the contents to about 173 degrees Fahrenheit (78 degrees Celsius) (the temperature at which alcohol boils). Open a window or a vent to provide proper ventilation of the fumes.

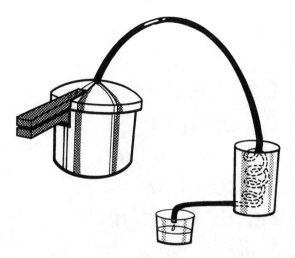

When the contents inside the pressure cooker are heated to about 173 degrees Fahrenheit (78 degrees Celsius), alcohol vapors running through the coils will condense within the coffee can containing ice and come out of the other end of the copper coil into a bowl or cup.

2. During this distillation process, the alcohol vapors running through the coils will condense within the coffee can filled with ice and come out of the other end of the copper coil into the bowl (see illustration). Measure the proof of this alcohol with the proof hydrometer and pour it back into the pot again to be distilled a second time in order to attain an even higher proof. Repeat this process until you have achieved the highest possible proof of alcohol from your still.

3. Measure the amount of alcohol fuel you have produced with the 2 gallons (7.6 liters) of mash. Use this figure to calculate how much alcohol fuel could be produced from what you estimate to be the average weekly household output of organic garbage.

4. Next, prepare four fuel-burning lamps that will each burn the same amount of alcohol, gasoline, benzene, and kerosene individually. Time the longevity of their flames to see which one lasts the longest. Note which one creates the least amount of smoke and odorous fumes.

Results

1. What was the highest proof you were able to obtain in your alcohol?

2. How much alcohol was produced from 2 gallons (7.6 liters) of mash? From your calculations, how much alcohol could be produced weekly from the organic garbage of an average household?

3. Which fuel burned the longest and most efficiently? How long would the average weekly household yield of alcohol last? Would this satisfy most of the household's energy needs? How does alcohol as a fuel source compare to the traditional fuels?

ENVIRONMENTAL SCIENCE

Can Earthworms Be Used to Recycle Kitchen Wastes into Fertile Garden Soil?

Purpose

To determine whether it is possible to establish a recycling system for household waste into fertile garden soil by means of earthworms.

Materials Needed

- scale
- 1 colony of red earthworms (approximately 100 worms)
- 3 ounces (84 grams) of cornmeal
- 14 pounds (6.3 kg) of nonfertilized regular lawn soil
- 10-gallon (19-liter) pail
- organic kitchen wastes (e.g., apple peelings, potato peelings, bread crumbs, etc.)

- preweighed container
- latex gloves
- newspaper
- 6 flower pots
- packets of seeds for three types of garden vegetables
- masking tape
- marking pen
- ruler

Experiment

A kitchen compost container will be created to establish and study the feasibility of an organic kitchen waste recycling system that will employ the use of red earthworms. The soil from this system will be compared with that of nonfertilized regular soil for overall quality in growing garden vegetables.

Procedure

1. Weigh the colony of earthworms in the soil that you received them in.
2. Mix the cornmeal into half of the soil in the pail which will serve as the kitchen compost container.
3. Place the worms on the surface of the soil. Once the worms have disappeared into the soil, weigh the unit and place the container in your basement or outside your backdoor.
4. Allow two or three days to pass in which to collect 2 cups (0.5 liter) of organic kitchen wastes. Place the wastes in a preweighed container, weigh the unit as a whole, subtract the weight of the container, and record the weight of the wastes. Add the wastes to the kitchen compost container. Continue to add 2 cups (0.5 liter) of weighed organic kitchen wastes to the compost container every two to three days for a two-month period. In order to determine which types of wastes are more acceptable to the worms, be sure to add a variety of wastes.
5. Weigh the entire compost container at the end of each week and keep a record of its weekly weight. Without disturbing the compost container, check it daily for signs of activity among the worms. Look for young worms and cocoons.
6. At the end of the two-month period, weigh the container and do not add any more kitchen wastes. Put on a pair of latex gloves, take the kitchen compost container into your backyard, and gently empty its contents over newspaper which has been laid over the ground. With your hands, separate most of the

Connecticut Science Fair finalist Frank Waluk and his project.

soil from the worms and divide it evenly between three flower pots. Divide the remaining nonfertilized regular soil between the remaining three flower pots.

7. Germinate the three types of garden vegetable seeds according to the packet instructions and plant some of them separately in the three labeled pots containing the kitchen compost soil. Then, plant some separately in the three labeled pots containing the remaining nonfertilized regular soil.

8. Observe the plants on a daily basis. Once they have sprouted, measure their growth every three days for a period of seven weeks. Note the rate of growth and overall quality of the plants. If time permits, monitor the complete growing cycle of the plants and the quality of the vegetables each one produces.

Results

1. What was the original weight of the kitchen compost container? What was the weight of the container at the end of the two-month period? Subtract the ending weight from the original weight. Does the difference equal the weight of the kitchen wastes that were added over the two-month period, or is it lower?

2. How did the weight of the kitchen compost container vary over the two-month period? Did it increase or remain constant during that time?

3. Was there more activity among the worms during the day or night? Did the worms accept some wastes more than others? What can the activity of the worms tell you about improving upon the kitchen compost container?

4. Which soil produced the best plants? vegetables?

5. Is the kitchen compost container an efficient system for recycling organic kitchen waste? Would the addition of another colony of worms make it more effective?

ENVIRONMENTAL SCIENCE

The Great American Lawn and Pristine Water: Can They Coexist?

Note: Safety goggles and gloves should be worn while handling the chemical reagents used in this experiment, which are considered hazardous substances.

Purpose

To determine how the amount of dissolved oxygen in pristine water, which is needed by fish and other water species for survival, is affected by man-made nutrients such as lawn fertilizers.

Materials Needed

- 3 2-ounce (60-ml) water sampling bottles
- distilled water
- 2-ounce (60-ml) water samples from 3 local bodies of water (e.g., lake, pond, and stream)
- 3 gallons (11.5 liters) of water from the same local bodies of water
- latex gloves

- safety goggles
- 6 pipettes
- manganous sulfate solution
- alkaline potassium iodide azide
- sulfamic acid powder
- titration kit
- 3 5-gallon (19-liter) fish tanks, sterilized
- ¼ teaspoon (2 g) each of 3 different lawn fertilizers

Experiment

Water samples from three pristine local bodies of water will be studied in their natural states to determine the amount of dissolved oxygen that they contain. Then, water samples will be drawn from the same bodies of water and transported into fish tanks where various lawn fertilizers will be introduced. These water samples will be studied to determine if the fertilizers have any effect on the amount of dissolved oxygen that was originally found to be present in the samples in their natural states.

Procedure

1. Select three local bodies of water that are situated in rural areas and are secure from possible contamination.

2. Sterilize the water sampling bottles with boiled distilled water before collecting the samples.

3. Fill a bottle with a water sample from each site by submerging it in the water and capping it while still submerged to be sure no air bubbles are trapped inside the bottle. Also collect 3 gallons of water (11.4 liters) from each site.

4. Put on the latex gloves and lab goggles to protect your hands and eyes in this part of the experiment. With a pipette, add eight drops of the manganous sulfate solution to the water sample, being careful not to introduce air into the water sample. With another pipette, add eight drops of alkaline potassium iodide azide to the same water sample, again being sure not to introduce any air into the sample. Cap the bottle and distribute the solution by turning the bottle around several times. After the precipitate forms, let it settle down from the top of the bottle. Add ⅛ teaspoon (1.0 g) of sulfamic acid powder and shake until the precipitate that is formed, as well as the sulfamic acid powder, are dissolved. When the sample becomes yellow- or amber-colored, it is ready for the dissolved oxygen test. Follow the instructions that come with the titration kit that you have obtained, and record the amount of dissolved oxygen for the sample.

5. Repeat steps 3 and 4 for the remaining water samples.

6. Pour one-third of the water that was obtained from the first site into a fish tank. Introduce one-half of one of the lawn fertilizers into the water. Once the fertilizer is dissolved, repeat steps 3 and 4 to determine the amount of dissolved oxygen in the sample and record your results.

7. Repeat step 6 twice, using a clean fish tank each time, to test the two remaining lawn fertilizers with the water remaining from the first site.

8. Empty and wash the fish tanks. Then repeat steps 6 and 7 for the water samples obtained from the second and third sites.

Results

1. Were the amounts of dissolved oxygen found to be the same between the three bodies of water? If not, what factors may have accounted for these differences?

2. Did any of the fertilizers affect the amount of dissolved oxygen originally noted for each sample? If so, would the presence of this fertilizer (in the same proportion as tested in this experiment) have any noticeable effects on the fish and other water species living in any of the tested sites?

19

Do Gas Stations Affect the Soil Around Them?

Purpose

To determine whether gas stations affect the soil around them by comparing the dominant types of soil microbes, as well as the pH level of soil samples, from the land around a typical gas station with those from land away from the gas station.

Materials Needed

- 8-ounce (224-g) soil samples from the land around three gas stations
- 8-ounce (224-g) soil samples from an urban, suburban, and rural area distant from a gas station
- distilled water
- 6 20-ml calibrated tubes with caps
- 6 sterile cotton swabs
- 6 petri dishes: tryptic soy agar with 5% sheep blood
- masking tape
- marking pen
- incubator
- Gram's stain test materials (see Project 37)
- camera
- sterile lab dish with depressions
- pH indicator
- 6 sterile plastic spatulas

Experiment

Soil samples from the land around three different gas station locations will be tested to determine whether bacterial growth from these samples differs from the bacterial growth from soil samples taken from urban, suburban, and rural areas away from the gas stations, which will serve as the controls. Then, the pH levels of the soil samples from the different locations will be determined by performing a pH indicator test.

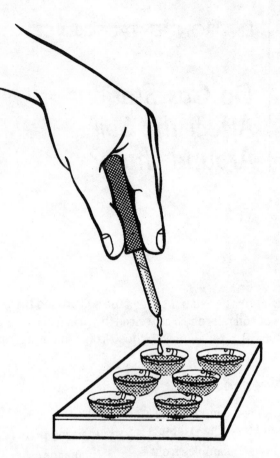

Once each of the soil samples has been placed in the lab dish and labeled, add enough pH indicator to each sample to be able to see the colors that form, and compare them to pH color standards.

Procedure

Part I

1. Place 1 ml of one gas station soil sample in a calibrated tube. Add 2 ml of distilled water and shake for 1 minute.

2. Dip a sterile cotton swab into the tube and streak the swab onto a petri dish. Label the dish and incubate it for 48 hours.

3. Remove the petri dish from the incubator, observe the bacterial growth, and make a Gram's stain (see steps 7 through 10 of Part I in Project 37) from the culture to determine whether the bacteria is gram-positive or gram-negative.

4. Record and photograph your results. Repeat steps 1 through 3 for the remaining gas station soil samples and the control soil samples. Compare your results.

Part II

1. Place a pea-sized portion of each soil sample into a separate depression of the lab dish to cover half the area of each depression, and label all.

2. Add pH indicator drops to each depression so that you can see the color that forms, in order to be able to compare it to the pH color standards (be careful not to flood the depressions). Stir each depression with a sterile spatula.

3. Tilt the lab dish to check the color of all the liquids, and record your pH findings. (The pH indicator will turn red in soil that is highly acidic and will turn blue to violet in soil that is highly alkaline.)

Results

1. Did the bacterial growth in the soil samples from the gas station sites differ from the bacterial growth of the control soil samples? Was the bacteria found to be gram-positive or gram-negative?

2. Which soil samples had the highest and lowest estimated pH levels?

3. What is the overall effect that gas stations appear to have on the soil around them?

What Is the Effect of #6 Heating Oil on Elodea densa *in an Aquatic Environment?*

Purpose

To determine the effects of a simulated oil spill on the flora in an aquatic environment.

Materials Needed

- 5 rinsed glass fishbowls
- clean gravel to cover the bottoms of 5 fishbowls
- 10 quarts (10 liters) distilled water
- 40 *Elodea densa* plants
- razor
- ruler
- fluorescent lamp
- microscope
- masking tape
- marking pen
- 500-ml beaker
- 375 ml #6 heating oil

Experiment

The plants will be divided into four experimental groups and one control group. The experimental groups will receive different concentrations of oil, while the control group will receive no oil. The plants will be allowed to adjust to their environments before the oil is administered to them in varying amounts. The reaction and appearance of the plants will be recorded through visual and microscopic observation.

Procedure

1. To each of the fishbowls add gravel to cover the bottom, and 2 quarts (liters) of distilled water.

2. Cut the plants with the razor to 4 inches (10 cm) in length. Separate the plants into five groups, eight plants in each group. Determine the number of stolons (the thread-like growth that branches off the stem) per plant and record the length of each. Record characteristics of color and general health in each plant group. Then, cut each stolon so that any new growth will be detected after experimentation.

3. Place the five plant groups deeply into the gravel of their designated bowls. Make sure that their leaves are not covered.

4. Place the bowls under a fluorescent lamp (each bowl should have the same lighting conditions). Allow the plants to adjust to their environment and root into the gravel for about a week.

5. Once the plants are established in their environment and all of the plants are rooted, begin to cut cross-sections from the plants and observe their inner cell structure under a microscope. Then place one plant from each group on a ruler and measure its average growth in height. Also record any differences in coloration among the plants.

6. Label the fishbowls according to the amount of #6 heating oil they will receive: 200 ml, 100 ml, 50 ml, 25 ml, and 0 ml (the control group). Then, measure the appropriate amounts of #6 heating oil with the beaker and add to each bowl.

7. Expose the plants to the oil for 6 days. Then remove the plants from each bowl and count the number of stolons, if any, and measure the plants to determine the amount of new growth. Cut cross-sections from them to observe their inner cell structure under a microscope. Record the results.

Results

1. At what point in the 6-day period did the plants begin to show any adverse reactions?

2. What changes did you observe, if any, in the cellular structure of the cross-sections before and after the oil was added?

3. Did any stolons reappear in any plant after the experiment?

4. What is the maximum amount of oil per 2 quarts (2 liters) of water that a simulated aquatic flora environment can tolerate and still survive? What does this imply about the fauna that coexist with and depend on such plants?

21

Can Limestone Be Used to Protect Pine Trees from Acid Rain?

Purpose

To determine if limestone, which is used to enrich soil so that grass and shrubbery may grow healthier, could protect pine trees from acid rain.

Materials Needed

- waterproof labels
- marking pen
- 4 potted pine trees [about 2 feet (60 cm) in height and all of the same age]
- 9 ounces (252 g) limestone (can be obtained from a garden supply store)
- tap water
- 3 quarts (2.9 liters) of a simulated acid rain solution (90% water/10% sulfuric acid)

Experiment

The soil of two potted pine trees will be fertilized with varying portions of limestone and then sprinkled with the simulated acid rain solution. Two other trees will serve as the controls, with one receiving the acid rain solution only and the other receiving limestone and regular water only. The acid rain solution will be given to the two experimental trees periodically for 4 weeks together with the limestone. The two controls will receive either the acid rain solution or limestone and water only.

Procedure

1. Label the trees as *Experimental 1, Experimental 2, Control 1,* and *Control 2.*

2. Apply ½ ounce (14 g) of limestone to the soil of *Experimental 1,* 1 ounce (28 g) to the soil of *Experimental 2,* and ¾ ounce (21 g) to *Control 1* (no limestone

will be given to *Control 2*). Each tree (with the exception of *Control 1*) will then be sprinkled with 4 ounces (120 ml) of the simulated acid rain solution.

3. One day each week, repeat the same doses of limestone you originally gave to the trees (except *Control 2*). Two days each week, give 4 ounces (120 ml) of the acid rain solution to the trees (except *Control 1*). Give the experimental trees their portion on the same day they will receive the limestone treatments Continue for four weeks.

4. Record the condition of the trees on a daily basis.

Results

1. What were the overall conditions of the plants after experimentation? Were the experimental trees that were treated with limestone in better condition than the control that was not?

2. Did the control that received only limestone and regular water appear healthy or damaged?

3. What combination of limestone ($\frac{1}{2}$ ounce or 1 ounce) per 4 ounces acid rain solution yielded the most favorable results?

22

What Section of a Town Has the Most Pollution in the Form of Airborne Particles?

Purpose

To determine which section of any given town contains the most airborne particles as pollution.

Materials Needed

- 30 3-by-5-inch (7.5-by-12.5-cm) index cards
- pencil
- petroleum jelly
- stapler
- 30 sticks of balsa wood or wooden dowels
- magnifying glass
- clear plastic wrap

Experiment

Index cards smeared with petroleum jelly will be used to collect samples of airborne particles from ten designated locations of a town. Three samples will be taken at each location under different types of weather conditions—dry and calm, windy, and hot and humid.

Procedure

1. Select ten test locations in a particular town and write the name of each location on three separate index cards.

2. Draw a circle on the index cards and smear them with petroleum jelly. Next, staple each card to a balsa wood stick and place each stick in the ground at each of the locations for 48 hours under dry and calm weather conditions.

3. After the 48 hours, collect all the sticks and count every particle within the circles using the magnifying glass. Record your results for each location, wrap the cards individually in the plastic wrap and store them carefully.

4. Repeat steps 2 and 3 under windy weather conditions and under hot and humid conditions. (If rainfall should occur, the samples must be retaken.) Record all your results.

5. After all the particle collections are made, average the three results for each location to arrive at a standard number for each particular site.

Results

1. Which site collected the most airborne particles under all three weather conditions?

2. Which type of the three weather conditions seemed to bring about the most airborne particles? The least?

3. Try to identify the airborne particles and their sources.

4. Did the airborne particles that were found in one location appear to be the same as those found in another location? If so, which type of particle seemed to be the most airborne?

5. In general, which section of the town had the most pollution?

23

Environmental Effects on the Biodegradability of Plastic Bags, Paper Bags, and Newspaper

Note: This experiment requires a time period of at least 3 months.

Purpose

To test several types of plastic bags in different environments to determine if and how fast they decompose in comparison to paper bags and newspaper in the same environments.

Materials Needed

- 10 biodegradable plastic bags (use two different brands)
- 10 nonbiodegradable plastic bags (use two different brands)
- 3 nets (plastic or cotton)
- wire or string
- 6 wooden posts
- 5 brown paper bags
- 5 pages of newspaper
- mulch pile—approximately 4 feet (120 cm) high (consisting of grass clippings and leaves with rotting vegetable matter, fertilizer, and compost starter culture) in a 6-foot- (2-m-) diameter ring made of wire fencing material
- tap water
- leaf pile—approximately 3 feet (1 m) high
- 10 plastic containers (approximately $\frac{1}{2}$ gallon (2 liters) each)
- saltwater (15% by volume)

Experiment

The biodegradability of several plastic bags, brown paper bags, and newspaper will be tested in different environmental conditions: in direct sunlight, in a mulch pile (to simulate an active landfill), in a leaf pile (to simulate a dry landfill), in tap water (to simulate a lake), and in saltwater (to simulate an ocean).

Procedure

1. Fold and secure two types of biodegradable plastic bags and two types of nonbiodegradable plastic bags on top of a net with wire or string. Tie a wooden post at each end of the net and place each post into the ground, leaving the plastic bags exposed to the sun. Do the same with one paper bag and a page of newspaper.

2. Repeat step 1 by placing the same types of bags in the middle of a mulch pile. Wet the pile thoroughly with water

3. Repeat step 1 by placing the same types of bags in the middle of the leaf pile.

4. Place two types of biodegradable plastic bags, two types of nonbiodegradable plastic bags, one paper bag, and one page of newspaper into five separate containers of tap water. Then, place the same types of materials into separate containers of 15% (by volume) saltwater.

5. Allow all the materials to stay in their environments for three months or longer. Record the changes that occurred to the plastic bags, paper bags, and newspapers in the different environments upon removal.

Results

1. Did any of the materials decompose? If so, which materials decomposed most thoroughly?

2. Was the rate of degradation greatest in the sunlight, mulch pile, leaf pile, tap water, or saltwater environments?

3. Did the plastic bags that were advertised as biodegradable appear any different from the nonbiodegradable bags?

ENVIRONMENTAL SCIENCE

24

How Does Acid Rain Affect the Cell Structure of Spirogyra?

Purpose

To determine whether water that contains a measurable level of acid—with a pH level below 7 (to simulate acid rain)—will affect the cellular structure of *Spirogyra*, a common freshwater algae of the phylum Chlorophyta.

Materials Needed

- 3 *Spirogyra* algae cultures
- 3 1-gallon (3.79-liter) fishbowls
- 6 quarts (liters) distilled water
- 1 quart (liter) soil/water mixture (5 mg soil and 1 quart (liter) tap water)
- 3 lamps, each with 40-watt bulb

- thermometer
- dropper (cc-calibrated)
- concave microscope slides
- 200× microscope
- pH indicator
- 15 cc of 90% water and 10% sulfuric acid

Experiment

Cultures of *Spirogyra* will be grown in three separate fishbowls. One will contain healthy algae cultivated in pollution-free water. Another will contain healthy algae cultivated in a low-acid water solution (water in which a small amount of acid solution is added to bring the pH to a level of 6.0). The third fishbowl will contain healthy algae cultivated in a high-acid water solution (water in which a greater amount of acid solution is added to bring the pH to a level of 3.0). Specimens from each tank will be drawn daily and observed with a 200× microscope. These observations will be recorded and labeled.

Procedure

1. Place equal amounts of *Spirogyra* cultures separately in the three fishbowls which should contain 2 quarts (liters) of distilled water. Then, add an equal amount of the soil/water mixture to each bowl to promote rapid algae growth. Place each bowl under a 40-watt lamp and heat to 68 degrees Fahrenheit (20 degrees Celsius).

2. Observe and record the algae growth daily.

Bowl 1 will be left with the neutral solution of water and healthy algae.

Bowl 2 will contain 3 cc of the water and 10% sulfuric acid solution to yield a low-acid solution with a pH of 6.0.

Bowl 3 will contain 12 cc of the water and 10% sulfuric acid solution to yield a high-acid solution with a pH of 3.0.

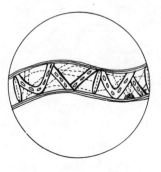

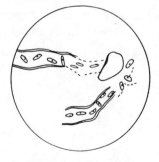

On day 3, the cell structure of the algae from Bowl 1 should be normal.

On day 3, the cell structure of the algae from Bowl 2 should show some signs of deterioration.

On day 3, the cell structure of the algae from Bowl 3 should be under complete destruction.

3. When the algae appear healthy and abundant, take a sample from each tank and observe it on slides under the microscope. Be sure to label the samples as to the specific bowl from which they were taken.

4. Allow the algae to grow under optimum laboratory conditions for ten days. On the tenth day, take another sample from each of the three bowls and observe them on slides under the microscope. Measure the pH level of the water, using the pH indicator. A neutral solution should be found in each bowl.

5. *Acid Rain Day 1:* The simulated acid rain will now be administered to the bowls. (Bowl 1 will be left with the neutral solution of water and healthy algae to serve as the control.) With the dropper, add 3 cc of the mixture of water and 10% sulfuric acid (to yield a pH of 6.0) into Bowl 2. Into Bowl 3, add 12 cc of the mixture of water and 10% sulfuric acid (to yield a pH of 3.0). Immediately take an algae sample from these two bowls for microscopic viewing, and draw and label the results.

6. *Acid Rain Day 2:* 24 hours after the simulated acid rain has entered the water supply of the *Spirogyra*, take samples of the algae again from each bowl (including the control) and observe them under the microscope. Note any changes in the algae cell structure. Draw and label what you see.

7. *Acid Rain Day 3:* 48 hours after the simulated acid rain has entered the water supply of the *Spirogyra,* take algae samples from each bowl (including the control) and observe them under the microscope. Note any increased cellular changes. Again, draw and label what you see.

8. Compare the differences in the cell structures between the three samples for the 3-day period.

Results

1. Locate a diagram of a typical, healthy *Spirogyra* cell. Is this diagram consistent with your final drawing of algae from Bowl 1? Compare this diagram with your final drawings from Bowls 2 and 3. Were there any changes at all in the structure of the algae? If so, what part of the algae's cellular structure has been altered?

2. What conclusions can be drawn from the effects that the simulated acid rain had on the *Spirogyra*? Was this simulation comparable to actual acid rain? What other acids might be used to simulate the rain?

25

The Presence of Heavy Metals in a Coastal Body of Water and Their Effect on Aquatic Life

An International Science and Engineering Fair Project

Note: This experiment must be conducted under the supervision of a research scientist and x-ray technician. The International Science and Engineering Fair has established strict guidelines to which all of its affiliate fairs must adhere. These guidelines involve experimentation with vertebrate animals and animal tissue. It is the responsibility of the student to follow these rules carefully. (See the Foreword and/or contact Science Service, the administrator of the ISEF, for a copy of the applicable rules.

Purpose

Since heavy metal pollution in marine environments is a problem in many coastal areas due to the discharge of industrial wastes, the objective of this research project is to determine the type and amount of heavy metal concentrations that exist and how they affect the development and health of fish at different sites along a given coastal body of water.

Materials Needed

- European beam trawl with 60-foot (18-m) line
- various fish species from sites along a coastal body of water
- large plastic freezer bags
- masking tape
- marking pen
- dissection instruments
- large glass lab vials
- 10% buffer solution (formalin phosphate)
- 10% nitric acid

- deionized water
- methylene chloride
- fume hood
- polyethylene scintillation vials with lids
- 120-ml microwave digestion bombs and Teflon liners
- digestive microwave oven
- 50-ml polypropylene centrifuge tubes
- 30% hydrogen peroxide
- flame atomic absorption spectrophotometer (Perkin-Elmer model 2380; AS 50 autosampler)
- X-ray machine
- dissecting microscope

Experiment

Random fish samples will be collected over a period of 12 months from various sites along a coastal body of water. Identification will be made of the species in each of the collection sites; tests for the presence of heavy metals in the fish samples will be conducted through use of an atomic absorption spectrophotometer; and the general health of the sampled fish will be assessed through studying their skeletal structures as well as their stomach and gill contents.

Procedure

Part I—Collect the fish samples.

1. Using the European beam trawl, take tows for five minutes at a time at five miles an hour along designated sites of a coastal body of water you have chosen and collect several samples of fish species (at least three of each species). Repeat procedure at various times during the year to collect a variety of species.

2. Preserve at least two fish from each species collected; place them in separate plastic bags, label the species name, date, and location found, and freeze immediately.

3. Remove the stomach and gills of one fish from each species and place into separately labeled vials containing the 10% buffer solution.

Part II—Dissect the fish and prepare tissue samples; perform atomic absorption spectrophotometry test.

1. Thaw one fish sample from each species.

2. Sterilize instruments before and after dissecting each sample by rinsing them with 10% nitric acid, deionized water, and methylene chloride.

3. With the assistance of a research scientist, perform dissections on each fish sample in a clean fume hood to obtain liver and muscle tissue. Place the tissues into separately labeled polyethylene scintillation vials that have been acid-soaked and rinsed in deionized water. If any fish species are too small for dissection, immerse their entire bodies into the vials.

4. Transfer all the tissue samples (including any whole-bodied samples) from the vials into the Teflon liners and the 120-ml microwave digestion bombs.

Add 1 teaspoon (5 ml) of nitric acid to each sample and allow the samples to de-gas for at least an hour.

5. Seal the bombs and place them in the digestive microwave oven until the samples are digested.

6. Remove the bombs from the oven, cool to room temperature, vent, and transfer the contents of each into separate centrifuge tubes. Then, bring the samples up to the 50-ml mark with ½ teaspoon (2.5 ml) of 30% hydrogen peroxide and deionized water.

7. With the assistance of a research scientist, analyze each prepared sample using the flame atomic absorption spectrophotometer to determine the presence and amount of metals such as copper, cadmium, manganese, zinc, silver, and iron.

Part III—Perform skeletal, gill, and stomach analysis.

1. With the assistance of an X-ray technician, have several radiographs taken of each species group. Analyze and compare the skeletal structures between fish from the same site. Analyze and compare the skeletal structures between fish from different sites. Record your results.

2. Remove the gills from the vials and examine them under the dissecting microscope for abnormalities. Record your results.

3. Remove the stomachs from the vials and check for exterior abnormalities. Then, take tissue cross-sections from the stomach samples and examine them under the dissecting microscope for abnormalities.

International Science and Engineering Fair award winner Nicole D'Amato found that the heavy metal concentrations in her fish samples from Long Island Sound were within the acceptable ranges established by the FDA.

Results

1. What fish species were you able to identify? Were the same species available at the same sites throughout the year?

2. What were the types and amounts of heavy metal concentrations found in the samples? Did they vary in samples taken from the same sites at different times of the year?

3. Did you find any abnormalities in the gills and stomachs of the samples?

26

What Substance Is Most Effective for Cleaning Teeth?

Note: The International Science and Engineering Fair has established strict guidelines to which all of its affiliate fairs must adhere. These guidelines involve experimentation with human and animal tissue. It is the responsibility of the student to follow these rules carefully. (See the Foreword and/or contact Science Service, the administrator of the ISEF, for a copy of the applicable rules.)

Purpose

To determine which tooth cleaner most effectively protects teeth from sugars and acids that dimineralize and decalcify tooth enamel.

Materials Needed

- 12 extracted molars (approximately the same age and in good condition, available from a dentist's office)
- water
- 12 empty petri dishes
- soda pop
- lemon juice
- toothbrush
- baking soda
- mouthwash
- fluoridated toothpaste
- nonfluoridated toothpaste
- tartar-control toothpaste

Experiment

Twelve different molars will be exposed to sugars and acids (soda pop and lemon juice) for a period of three weeks. Each of ten teeth will be cleaned daily with one of the cleaners. The two remaining teeth will serve as the control and will be brushed with water only. At the end of three weeks the condition of the molars will be carefully observed to determine which substance worked the best as a cleaner and provided the greatest protection.

Procedure

1. Rinse the teeth with boiling water and dry them thoroughly.
2. Fill six empty petri dishes three-fourths full with soda pop. Then fill the other six empty petri dishes three-fourths full with lemon juice.
3. Place a molar into each dish, cover it, and label it according to the type of cleaning solution with which it will be brushed. For example, begin by labeling one molar in the soda pop solution *SP—baking soda* and one molar in the lemon juice solution *LJ—baking soda,* and so on.
4. Soak each tooth in its solution for 24 hours. Then remove the teeth individually and brush them with the substance that is labeled on their particular dishes. After cleaning, return the teeth to their petri dishes, cover, and repeat the same procedure daily for three weeks. At the end of the period observe the condition of each tooth. Look for signs of deterioration and discoloring.

Results

1. Did any of the teeth show signs of deterioration and discoloring? If so, what changes did you observe? Were these changes consistent among all the teeth, or did they vary?
2. Which substance, soda pop or lemon juice, had the greatest impact, if any, on the molars?
3. Which substance, if any, kept the teeth clean and protected the longest? Does this result agree or disagree with what your dentist recommends as a tooth cleaner?

27

The Relationship Between Alcohol Dosage and Dependency in a Rat

Note: This experiment must be conducted under the supervision of a licensed veterinarian or research scientist. The International Science and Engineering Fair has established strict guidelines to which all of its affiliate fairs must adhere. These guidelines involve experimentation with vertebrate animals. It is the responsibility of the student to follow those rules carefully. (See the Foreword and/ or contact Science Service, the administrator of the ISEF, for a copy of the applicable rules.)

Purpose

To determine the effects of various, physically tolerable levels of alcohol exposure in rats by analyzing their behavioral responses and related blood alcohol levels.

Materials Needed

- 4 airtight inhalation chambers
- oxygen and ethanol/oxygen vaporization, metering, and pumping equipment.
- food and water for the rats
- 12 laboratory rats
- enzyme assay equipment (for determining the blood-alcohol levels in the rats)
- trichloroacetic acid
- Ependorf tubes
- microcentrifuge
- alcohol dehydrogenase and nicotinamide adenine dinucleotide
- glycine buffer
- timer
- spectrophotometer

Experiment

Twelve rats will be divided into three groups of four and placed individually in airtight inhalation chambers. Three rats from each group will be exposed to a controlled rate of alcohol vaporization (the experimental group), while the remaining rat will not (the control rat). Over a period of time, blood samples will be obtained from the tail veins of each rat and an enzyme assay test will be conducted to determine the average blood-alcohol level in each rat. After the rats have been exposed for 3 days, they will be removed from their environments. About 6 hours later, the withdrawal symptoms of the rats will be observed for tail tremors, tail stiffening, body tremors, and body rigidity. The experiment will be repeated on Groups 2 and 3 at higher levels of alcohol vaporization.

Procedure

1. Obtain permission to work under the supervision of a research scientist, probably at a local university.

2. Set up the inhalation chambers and connect the ethanol/oxygen vaporization equipment to three chambers, while connecting the fourth chamber to equipment that will vaporize only oxygen. Be sure to supply food and water for each chamber.

3. Place one rat into each of the four chambers and administer the ethanol/oxygen vaporization and the oxygen vaporization.

4. Keep the rats in their chambers with food and water for 3 days. During this period obtain 100 μl of blood from the tail veins of each rat each day with the help of the research scientist and derive the average blood-alcohol level of each rat through the enzyme assay procedure.

5. To complete the enzyme assay procedure, first deproteinize each blood sample by adding 400 μl of trichloroacetic acid to each blood sample in an Ependorf tube. Spin the Ependorf tube for 4 minutes in a microcentrifuge. This will separate the sample into protein and plasma.

6. Place 100 μl of the plasma into a prepared assay vial containing alcohol dehydrogenase and nicotinamide adenine dinucleotide. Add 3 ml of glycine buffer to the vial. Invert the vial and allow it to sit for 30 minutes.

7. Place the vial in a spectrophotometer and set the visible light wavelength to 340 nm. The higher the alcohol content in the vial, the lower the light emission when placed in the spectrophotometer. These measurements will result in a reading that translates to the appropriate percentage of blood-alcohol level.

8. After the third day, remove and separate the first group of experimental rats and the control rat. Compare all symptoms of nervousness and withdrawal immediately and after a 6-hour period.

9. Repeat the same procedures for the second and third groups of rats. However, Group 2 should be exposed to a slightly higher amount of ethanol vapors than Group 1, and Group 3 should be exposed to a slightly higher amount of ethanol vapors than Group 2.

David Karanian found that even low levels of blood-alcohol were sufficient to generate alcohol dependency in the rats as measured by their withdrawal symptoms over a 3-day period.

Results

1. What physical changes were visible in each rat after alcohol exposure? After 6 hours? Were there any noticeable differences between the experimental and the control groups?

2. What was the average blood-alcohol level in each rat? In a particular group? In the entire experimental group?

3. Were there variations among the blood-alcohol levels of the rats?

4. What percentage of blood-alcohol was needed over a 3-day period in order to generate dependency in the rats as measured by withdrawal symptoms?

5. Do you believe from this experiment that it was the amount of ethanol vaporization administered or the continuous exposure to the alcohol over the 3 days that was related to dependency?

6. Can you apply your findings to humans?

28

How Effective Are Various Items in Protecting against Ultraviolet Radiation?

Purpose

To use an organism such as a bacterium to simulate a human body in order to determine the effectiveness of items commonly used to protect against ultraviolet radiation.

Materials Needed

- sterile cotton swabs
- nutrient broth culture of bacteria (*Serratia marcescens*)
- 5 tryptic soy agar plates with 5% sheep blood (more plates will be needed if more than three items will be tested)

- various items used to protect the body against ultraviolet radiation, such as clothing, sunglasses, and sunscreen lotion
- ultraviolet lamp
- timer
- large lid

Experiment

Tryptic soy agar (TSA) plates with 5% sheep blood will be smeared with the bacteria *Serratia marcescens* and allowed to cultivate. Various items to be tested, such as clothing, sunglasses, and sunscreen lotion, will be placed over the bacteria as a protective covering from the ultraviolet radiation that the plates will be exposed to.

After the nutrient agar plates are covered with the bacteria, items normally used in the sun (such as sunglasses) will be placed on each plate to determine if they can actually protect the bacteria from the ultraviolet rays.

Procedure

1. With a sterile cotton swab, place the culture of bacteria on the entire surface of each of the five TSA plates and allow it to cultivate.

2. Cover the entire surface (if possible) of the three experimental plates with the items being tested—for example, clothing, glasses, and sunscreen. To do the sunscreen test, first smear the lotion on clear plastic wrap and then wrap the plastic over the plate. Leave two plates uncovered to serve as the control (one plate will be unexposed to the ultraviolet lamp, while the other will be exposed to the ultraviolet lamp).

3. Place the three experimental plates plus one of the uncovered control plates directly underneath the ultraviolet lamp for 5 minutes of exposure. Then turn off the light and remove the coverings from each dish. Cover these four exposed plates and the unexposed plate with a lid and put the plates away in a dark area at room temperature overnight.

4. Observe the condition of the bacteria after 24 hours and record your observations.

Results

1. Compare the population and color of the bacteria on the experimental plates exposed to ultraviolet light to that of the control plates. Is there any difference between the protected and exposed plates, or between the unprotected/exposed and unprotected/unexposed plates?

2. Which item offered the most protection against ultraviolet radiation? Which offered the least?

3. Compare colored and colorless testing items. Did the colored items have any effect on ultraviolet penetration? Compare the thickness of the materials. Did

thicker testing materials offer better protection against the ultraviolet radiation than thinner materials?

4. Did the sunscreen lotion offer good protection? Based on the data from this experiment, do you think that most people are well protected against ultraviolet radiation?

MATHEMATICS

The Wave, the Golden Mean, and $r = \left[\dfrac{2}{\left(-1+\sqrt{5}\right)}\right]^{\wedge}\theta$

An International Science and Engineering Fair Project

Note: Knowledge and experience in analytical geometry, origami, and computer programming are required for this project.

Purpose

To determine if there is any possible relationship between the origami fold known as the "wave" and the Golden Mean or Ratio, the numerical value of which is $\left(\frac{1+\sqrt{5}}{2}\right)$. This will be accomplished by determining the equation of the wave's spirals.

Materials Needed

- several sheets of 1-foot- (30-cm-) square origami paper (or more)
- 1 sheet of 20-inch- (50-cm-) square origami paper
- ruler
- 2 sheets of graph paper

- personal computer with 2 megabytes of memory
- software for writing a program that will create and calculate geometric and trigonometric figures and calculations

Experiment

The origami paper will be folded into patterns known as "waves." Each pattern will use a different number of divisions to demonstrate the effects of this on the resulting model. A geometric analysis will be performed to derive equations that describe characteristics of the folded models. Measurements of the models will be taken to be used as data to be related by polar equations. A basic program will be written on a personal computer with the use of software, to draw polar spirals of the logarithmic or equiangular variety, which will be adjusted to match the spirals found in the wave.

Procedure

1. Fold a smaller sheet of paper following the instructions in the diagram, each time using 3, 6, and 12 divisions. Observe the effect this has on the resolution and shape of the model. Try folding another small sheet with an uneven number of divisions (for example, 16ths at the point, moving to 8ths at the outer edges). Record your observations.

2. Carefully examine the structure of the resulting folds. Derive equations for the angles between consecutive secants of each spiral, as a function of the number of the division from the tip of the "wave," taking the tip to be fold #0. Try to use these equations to determine a polar equation describing the spirals.

3. Practice folding the "wave" a few more times. Then, fold a model using 32 divisions with the larger paper. If necessary, use a ruler to make straight creases.

4. Create a polar axis in the center of one of the sheets of graph paper. Draw a radius every .25π radians of rotation. Taking the point of the "wave" as the origin, trace the outline of the outer spiral of the "wave" onto the paper. Measure and record the radius length along each of the radii previously drawn.

5. Graph the measurements, using the angle as the x axis and the radius as the y

International Science and Engineering Fair finalist Matthew Green and his project.

The Wave

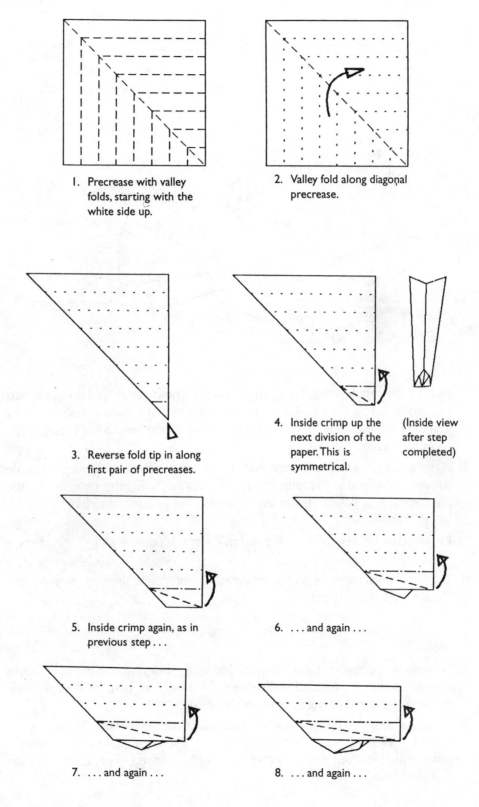

1. Precrease with valley folds, starting with the white side up.

2. Valley fold along diagonal precrease.

3. Reverse fold tip in along first pair of precreases.

4. Inside crimp up the next division of the paper. This is symmetrical.

   (Inside view after step completed)

5. Inside crimp again, as in previous step . . .

6. . . . and again . . .

7. . . . and again . . .

8. . . . and again . . .

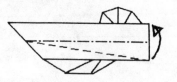

9. ... and again ...

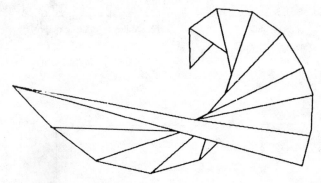

10. Valley fold down the flaps.

The "wave" model completed

axis, on the graph paper. Using the resulting graph, try to fit the results into an equation. Test the equations by graphing them in the same fashion, or by graphing them as polar equations and comparing the results to the actual spiral of the "wave."

6. Write a program with software that draws polar spirals, with user-definable constants. Include logarithmic spirals as an option. Using this program, adjust the constants to determine the equation that most closely matches that of the spiral of the "wave."

7. Express the best equation in logarithmic form: $ln(r) = k\theta$ and $r = c^{\theta}$, where k and c are constants.

8. Through observation and experimentation, determine the angular rotations between the three spirals.

Results

1. Describe your observations when folding with a different number of divisions and with an uneven number of divisions. What were the results? Was the basic shape of the spiral changed or unchanged? Why?

2. What were the three equations for the angles between secants? Were they the same for all three spirals? Why or why not? Were you able to determine a polar equation from your results? If so, did it show any connection to the Golden Mean?

3. What did the measurements show about the relationship between angle and radius? What type of equation seems to best approximate the measurements? Was there any noticeable relationship to the Golden Mean? What are the disadvantages of using this method?

4. Were you able to find an equation that produced a spiral similar to those in the "wave"? What was the final result? Is there any relationship to the Golden Mean? Can you prove it?

5. What were the rotations between the inner and outer spirals? How could you see this without drawing the graphs? What were the rotations between the outer and middle spirals?

6. What other observations or conclusions can you make? Are there any additional connections to the Golden Mean?

MICROBIOLOGY

30

Are Dandelions as Effective as Commonly Prescribed Antibiotics against Bacteria?

Purpose

To determine whether dandelion roots, which are used in many parts of the world for therapeutic purposes, can be used as an antibiotic against the bacteria *Serratia marcescens* and *Escherichia coli*, and to determine whether they are as effective as commonly prescribed antibiotics.

Materials Needed

- dandelion roots
- food processor
- cheesecloth
- 5 cups
- sterile distilled water
- dandelion capsules (can be obtained from a health food store)
- sterile pin
- penicillin tablets (250 mg) (can be obtained from a medical doctor)
- Erythromycin tablets (250 mg) (can be obtained from a medical doctor)
- Tetracycline tablets (250 mg) (can be obtained from a medical doctor)
- sterile applicators
- 12 petri dishes: tryptic soy agar with 5% sheep's blood
- *Serratia marcescens* culture
- *Escherichia coli* culture
- masking tape
- marking pen
- incubator
- forceps
- sterile filter paper disks

126

Experiment

Tests will be carried out to determine whether dandelion roots can be used as effective antibiotics. Dandelion roots taken directly from the ground as well as dandelion root capsules will be tested on selected bacteria to see if they have any effect. Control tests will also be conducted using three common antibiotics as well as distilled water on the same bacteria. The results of both tests will be analyzed and compared.

Procedure

Part I—Prepare the dandelion and the antibiotic
tablet solutions.

1. Thoroughly wash several dandelion roots and pulverize them in the food processor until they are liquefied.
2. Filter the liquefied roots through the cheesecloth and into a sterile cup. Add enough distilled water to the liquid to form a one-to-one ratio.
3. Pierce one dandelion capsule with a sterile pin and squeeze the contents into another cup holding ½ cup (0.12 liter) of distilled water.
4. Dissolve one penicillin tablet in ½ cup (0.12 liter) of water. Similarly, dissolve one Erythromycin and one Tetracycline tablet separately into ½ cup (0.12 liter) of water.

Part II—Test the solutions on the bacteria strains.

1. With a sterile applicator, streak six tryptic soy agar (TSA) petri dishes with the *Serratia marcescens*. With another sterile applicator and six TSA petri dishes, repeat this procedure with the *Escherichia coli*. Label the dishes and incubate them for 48 hours at 95 degrees Fahrenheit (35 degrees Celsius). Carefully note the growth of bacteria in each dish.
2. Using the forceps, dip a sterile filter paper disk into the dandelion root solution and place it onto one of the petri dishes containing *S. marcescens*. Dip another sterile filter paper disk into the dandelion capsule solution and place it onto the second petri dish containing *S. marcescens*. Continue this procedure by placing sterile filter paper disks soaked in the three antibiotic solutions onto the next three petri dishes containing *S. marcescens*. Place a sterile filter paper disk soaked only in sterile distilled water onto the remaining dish containing *S. marcescens*. Label all dishes accordingly.
3. Repeat step 2 with those dishes containing *E. coli*.
4. Incubate all the petri dishes for 48 hours at 95 degrees Fahrenheit (35 degrees Celsius). Carefully note the amount of bacteria in each dish and compare those results against the amount of bacteria found in each dish before it was treated. Compare the amount of bacteria between those dishes treated with the dandelion solutions to those treated with the antibiotic solutions and the untreated dishes. Record your observations.

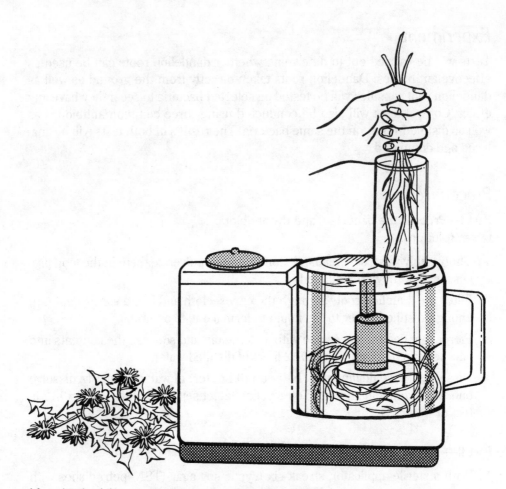

After the dandelion roots are separated from the flowers and stems, wash them thoroughly and pulverize them in the food processor.

Results

1. Were either the dandelion root or capsule solutions effective in inhibiting bacterial growth? If so, did their effectiveness vary with the type of bacteria used? Was one dandelion solution more effective than the other?

2. Were the antibiotic tablets successful in inhibiting the growth of the bacteria used in the experiment?

3. How did the dandelion solutions compare to the antibiotic solutions?

31

Can Food Molds Be Used to Reduce Bacteria Spread by a Pet Rabbit?

Note: This experiment must be conducted under the supervision of a licensed veterinarian or research scientist. The International Science and Engineering Fair has established strict guidelines to which all of its affiliate fairs must adhere. These guidelines involve experimentation with vertebrate animals. It is the responsibility of the student to follow these rules carefully. (See the Foreword and/ or contact Science Service, administrator of the ISEF, for a copy of the applicable rules.)

Purpose

To determine if food molds can control the growth of different types of bacteria taken from a pet rabbit.

Materials Needed

- white bread
- plastic bags
- fruit (e.g., cantaloupe)
- Roquefort cheese
- sterile applicators
- bacteria samples taken from a pet rabbit's ears, eyes, and feces
- 15 petri dishes: tryptic soy agar with 5% sheep blood
- masking tape
- marking pen
- 12 sterile spatulas
- antibacterial soap
- incubator

Experiment

Bacteria cultures from the ears, eyes, and feces of a pet rabbit will be analyzed and treated with various food molds to see if the molds can stop the growth of the bacteria. Part of the cultures will also be treated with antibacterial soap only and will be left alone to serve as the controls.

Procedure

1. Take several pieces of white bread, dampen lightly, and put them into a plastic bag. Similarly, cut a piece of fruit (such as a cantaloupe), in half and place one half into a plastic bag. Put the Roquefort cheese aside. Keep all of the food in a warm location and allow it to grow mold.

2. With the help of a licensed veterinarian or research scientist, obtain a bacteria sample with a sterile applicator from around one of the rabbit's ears and streak it onto five of the petri dishes. Repeat the procedure with samples from under the rabbit's eyes and from the rabbit's feces. Label all 15 dishes accordingly.

3. With one of the spatulas, evenly apply a layer of the mold from the white bread to cover the bacteria sample taken from around the rabbit's ear. Repeat the procedure for the samples taken from the rabbit's eyes and feces. Repeat the entire procedure using the molds taken from the fruit and the Roquefort cheese. Three of the six remaining samples will not be treated and will serve as the control set. The last samples will be treated with antibacterial soap.

4. Label and cover all petri dishes and place them in the incubator for 72 hours. Remove the dishes and observe the effects of the food molds and the antibacterial soap, if any, on the treated dishes.

Results

1. Did the food molds have any effect at all in preventing the growth of bacteria? If so, which one was the most effective?

2. If the molds were equally effective, which sample did they have the most antibacterial effect on?

3. How did the food molds compare to the antibacterial soap in inhibiting the growth of bacteria?

32

What Substance Is Most Effective for Preventing the Breeding of Bacteria in Waterbeds?

Purpose

To determine whether bacteria are present inside waterbeds and whether commercial waterbed conditioners or other disinfectants are effective in counteracting any organisms that may live inside.

Materials Needed

- large dropper
- test tubes
- water specimens from new and used waterbeds
- masking tape
- marking pen
- sterile applicators
- petri dishes: tryptic soy agar with 5% sheep blood, and MacConkey
- incubator
- API biochemical test manual
- several brands of waterbed conditioners
- several brands of household disinfectants
- warm tap water
- sterile cups
- sterile filter paper disks

Experiment

Specimens will be taken from both new and used waterbeds. These samples will be streaked individually onto separate tryptic soy agar (TSA) petri dishes, incubated, and observed for bacteria. If present, the bacteria will then be streaked onto MacConkey petri dishes, incubated, and observed for the presence of gram-negative bacteria, which will then be identified through the use of an API biochemical test. Following this step, the waterbed specimens will be streaked again onto another group of TSA petri dishes, and sterile filter paper disks that have each been dipped into a different type of waterbed conditioner and disinfectant will be placed on top of the dishes. The petri dishes will be incubated for 48 hours, and the effectiveness of the conditioners and disinfectants will be assessed.

Procedure

1. Using a large dropper and test tubes, collect water samples from inside several waterbeds and label them to indicate the age and make of each bed they were taken from. Using a sterile applicator, streak a portion of each onto a separate TSA petri dish, cover, label, and incubate them for 48 hours to determine if and how much bacteria are present. Compare and record your observations. If bacteria are present, streak the bacteria from each particular dish onto a corresponding MacConkey dish to determine the presence of gram-negative bacteria, which will be identified by an API biochemical test. API test instructions can be found in an API biochemical test manual.

2. Streak another portion of each specimen onto more TSA petri dishes. Prepare a solution of each brand of waterbed conditioner and disinfectant by diluting each separately in a solution of 1 part chemical to 5 parts water in sterile cups. Next, dip each of several sterile filter paper disks into a separate solution and place them individually on top of separate dishes (leave one dish untreated to serve as the control). Cover each dish and incubate for 48 hours.

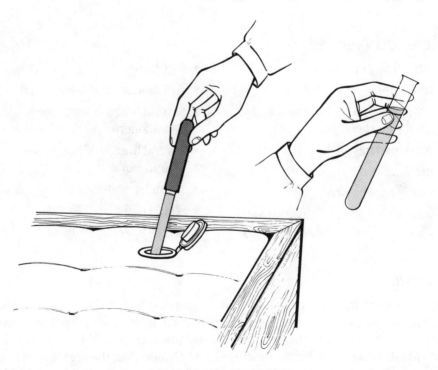

Remove water samples from each waterbed with a large dropper and put them into individual test tubes.

3. Remove the filter paper disks to see if the conditioners and disinfectants had any effect in reducing or eliminating the amount of bacteria that were present. This can be observed by measuring the clear zones found within the area in which the disks were placed on the petri dishes.

Results

1. What types of bacteria were found in the waterbeds? Were any pathogenic?
2. Did the age or make of the waterbeds influence the amount and type of bacteria found in them, or were all the beds consistent?
3. Was the amount of bacteria present in the petri dishes reduced or eliminated as a result of the treated filter paper disks?
4. Of all the chemicals used, which would be the best to keep a waterbed free of organisms?

33

How Can the Amount of Bacteria Found on Kitchen Sponges and Dishcloths Be Reduced?

Purpose

To discover which of several materials used to clean kitchen utensils, and the locations in which this material is kept, will harbor the most bacteria. To determine the measures to be taken in order to reduce most of the bacteria found in the materials after use.

Materials Needed

- masking tape
- marking pen
- 18 petri dishes: tryptic soy agar with 5% sheep blood
- 2 new kitchen sponges
- 2 new dishcloths
- 2 new dish mops

- 18 sterile cotton swabs
- 18 plastic bags
- camera
- 18 soiled eating utensils
- soapy tap water
- boiled water

Experiment

A variety of materials commonly used to wash eating utensils will be tested to see the amounts of bacteria each will contain after use. Several methods of reducing this bacteria before and after use will be tried and compared for effectiveness. The locations in which these materials are kept will also be tested to see which environment is ideal for reducing the amount of bacteria that can be acquired by the materials.

Procedure

1. Label 2 petri dishes for each one of the dishwashing materials. Next, rub a moistened sterile cotton swab across each material and streak it onto its marked petri dish. Cover the petri dishes and put them into plastic bags at room temperature for 24 hours, and then photograph each dish.

2. Divide the soiled utensils into six groups (each group will be washed with a different material). Proceed to wash one group of the utensils with one of the sponges. Then, rinse the sponge with soapy tap water, squeeze it out, and rub another sterile cotton swab across its surface. Streak the cotton swab onto its labeled petri dish, and cover. Then, wash another group of dirty utensils with the other sponge, rinse that sponge with boiled water, and squeeze it out. Rub a cotton swab over its surface, streak it onto another marked petri dish, and cover. Place both dishes into plastic bags at room temperature and photograph each after 24 hours.

3. Repeat step 2 with the remaining groups of utensils and dishwashing materials. Then, analyze each of the petri dishes to determine which material provided the best environment for bacterial growth and which rinsing method eliminated or counteracted the proliferation of bacteria.

4. For the second part of the experiment, place each material in a separate area of your kitchen immediately after being used in the first part of the experiment. (Possible locations include: underneath the sink, on the back of the stove top, on the counter top, and on the back of the sink top.) Allow the materials to stay in their locations for 24 to 48 hours, rub a cotton swab across their surfaces, and then streak each onto a specially marked petri dish. Again, cover the dishes and put them into plastic bags at room temperature. Observe your results.

Results

1. Did any of the dishwashing materials contain any bacterial contamination before they were used?

2. Which material provided the best environment for the bacteria to grow?

3. Which rinsing method appeared to be the most effective in either eliminating or reducing the amount of bacteria present after washing?

4. Did the storage of the sponges, dishcloths, or dish mops have any influence on the amount of bacteria present in the materials 24 to 48 hours after use?

5. What do your results imply about the cleanliness of utensils even after they are washed?

34

An Analysis of the Bacteria and Heavy Metal Content of Sewage Before and After Treatment at a Sewage Plant

Purpose

To analyze and compare the bacteria and heavy metal content of sewage from several sewage plants before treatment, and to determine what effects the treatment had on the sewage by analyzing and comparing bacteria and heavy metal content after treatment.

Materials Needed

- sterile wooden applicator sticks
- samples of untreated raw sewage and effluent from several treatment plants
- samples of the same type of sewage and effluent after treatment
- petri dishes: tryptic soy agar (TSA) with 5% sheep blood,

- colistin nalidixic acid (CNA), and MacConkey
- incubator
- API biochemical test manual
- sterile test tubes
- buffer reagent
- dithizone solution reagent

Experiment

Both raw and treated samples of the same type of sewage will be obtained from several sewage treatment plants. TSA petri dishes will first be used to determine the amount of bacteria present in the raw sewage. Then, CNA petri dishes which grow only gram-positive bacteria and MacConkey petri dishes which grow only gram-negative bacteria will be used. API tests will then be administered to identify the types of gram-negative bacteria present. Finally, the presence of heavy metals will be noted with the use of buffer and dithizone solution reagents. The experiment will then be repeated with the sewage samples after treatment.

Procedure

1. Place sterile wooden applicators into each untreated sample, streak them onto individual TSA petri dishes, label, and incubate them for 48 hours. After incubation, analyze the dishes to record the amount of bacteria present.

2. Repeat step 1 using CNA petri dishes, which grow only gram-positive bacteria, and again using MacConkey dishes, which grow only gram-negative bacteria. Incubate the dishes for 48 hours and then record the amount of bacterial growth in all the dishes.

3. Conduct the API tests (you will need to follow the instructions found in an API manual) to identify the types of gram-negative bacteria present in the MacConkey dishes.

4. To determine the amount of heavy metals, if any, present within the untreated sewage samples, put 2 teaspoons (10 ml) of each sample's effluent into individual test tubes. Add 0.1 of the buffer reagent and 1.6 ml of the dithizone reagent to each, and shake vigorously. A noticeable change in the color of the effluents will indicate the presence of heavy metals.

5. Repeat steps 1 through 4 with the treated sewage samples from the same plants. Record, analyze, and compare your results to the untreated samples to see if the bacteria or heavy metal content has decreased.

Results

1. Compare the types of bacteria found at each site. What type of bacteria was the most common among the different plants?

2. Were the bacteria found to be gram-negative or gram-positive? If gram-negative, what types of bacteria were identified?

3. Were heavy metals found in the effluent of any sewage samples? What did this indicate about the types of industries that use the particular sewage plant from which the samples came?

4. Did the treatment of the sewage decrease or alter the state of the bacteria and/or the heavy metals present?

Are Your Clams Safe to Eat?

Purpose

To determine if clams purchased fresh from local fish markets—as opposed to those that have gone through a depuration process at a purification plant—are safe to eat.

Materials Needed

- masking tape
- marking pen
- 6 clams each from fish markets in about 10 different regions
- sterile steaming pan
- timer
- sterile knife
- blender (with sterile container)
- sterile applicators
- petri dishes: tryptic soy agar with 5% sheep blood
- incubator
- photographed petri dishes of depured raw and steamed clams (as a control)

Experiment

Clams from different geographical areas that have not been depured will be bacteria-tested in both a raw and a cooked state to observe and compare the fecal bacteria counts to those of photographed petri dishes of depured clams.

Procedure

1. Label the groups of clams as to the areas from which each group came.
2. Take three clams of one group and steam them in the pan for 5 minutes. Then, open them with the knife and put their contents together in the blender; process for 90 seconds.
3. Using a sterile applicator, streak the blend onto a petri dish and incubate for 24 hours.
4. Repeat the blending and streaking procedure using the remaining three clams from the group. Do not steam them.

Brian Curtin bacteria-tested raw and depured clams from different geographical areas to determine if they were safe to eat.

5. Repeat steps 2 through 4 with clams from the other geographical groups.

6. Compare the results from each group to the photographed (control) petri dishes of both raw and steamed clams that have gone through the depuration process at a purification plant.

7. Identify the types and levels of bacteria present, and find out the levels at which they can be safely consumed.

Results

1. How does the bacteria count of the raw clams compare to that of the steamed clams? Did steaming in fact kill the bacteria? Are the raw clams safe to eat?

2. How did the bacteria count of the clams compare from market to market? From market to control (depured)?

3. Were all the bacteria that were found in the clams harmful?

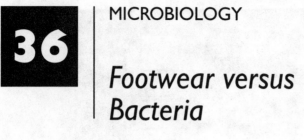

MICROBIOLOGY

36

Footwear versus Bacteria

Purpose

To determine whether footwear provides an environment for the growth of bacteria, and if so, to discover which type of footwear grows the most bacteria.

Materials Needed

- 10 different types of footwear (one pair from 10 different people)
- sterile applicators
- sterile water
- petri dishes: tryptic soy agar (TSA) with 5% sheep blood, colistin nalidixic acid (CNA), and MacConkey
- incubator
- masking tape
- marking pen
- clock
- camera

Experiment

A variety of footwear worn by ten different people will be used for the first part of the experiment to determine whether significant amounts of bacteria grew during the time they were worn. TSA petri dishes will be used. Then, the type of bacteria that grew most abundantly (gram-positive or gram-negative) will be identified, and the kind of footwear that provided the most ideal conditions for its growth will be determined. This will be done with CNA and MacConkey petri dishes.

Procedure

1. Swab the inside of each shoe or sneaker, before it is worn, with a sterile applicator moistened with sterile water. Streak a separate TSA petri dish with each applicator. Incubate the petri dishes for 48 hours. After incubation, analyze the dishes to determine the amount of bacterial growth. Be sure to label with the names of the individuals who will wear those particular shoes. This procedure will serve as a control for the experiment.

2. After the shoes and sneakers have been worn for 5 hours, swab the inside of each with moist sterile applicators. Then streak each applicator on individual TSA petri dishes. Again, be sure to label the dishes. Incubate the petri dishes for 48 hours and observe them.

3. After incubating the experimental petri dishes, compare them with their corresponding control petri dishes to see whether there were substantial increases in the amount of bacteria present.

4. Swab the inside of the same ten shoes with moist sterile applicators and streak each on CNA petri dishes, which grow only gram-positive bacteria, and on MacConkey petri dishes, which grow only gram-negative bacteria. Again, be sure to label the dishes. Then, incubate the dishes for 48 hours. After incubation, compare the bacterial growth between all the dishes and photograph each dish.

Results

1. Did the use of the footwear for the 5-hour period increase the amount of bacteria present before the experiment?

2. Which type of footwear provided the best environment for the growth of bacteria?

3. Was there any type of footwear that grew little or no bacteria?

4. What type of bacteria grew more abundantly—gram-negative or gram-positive? What does this tell you about the type of bacteria present?

5. What type of footwear seems to be the best to wear? The worst?

Swab the inside of a shoe or sneaker with a moist sterile applicator before it has been worn, and streak the applicator onto TSA petri dishes. Repeat this step after the footwear has been worn for 5 hours, streaking the applicators onto CNA and MacConkey petri dishes as well.

37

The P-Trap: A Bacteria Cauldron

An International Science and Engineering Fair Project

Purpose

To investigate the P-trap (the U-shaped pipe located underneath a sink) in various households, to determine:

1. Whether P-traps are vehicles conducive for the growth of bacteria.
2. Whether such bacteria could be harmful to humans.
3. What products could be used to prevent the growth of bacteria at such sites.

Materials Needed

- inoculating loop
- matches
- 20 different household sinks
- petri dishes: tryptic soy agar (TSA) with 5% sheep blood, and MacConkey
- incubator
- clock
- Gram's stain test materials: glass slides, bunsen burner, crystal

violet solution, tap water, iodine solution, 95% ethanol, safranine, microscope with oil-immersion lens
- sterile filter paper disks
- sterile forceps
- a variety of liquid and solid household cleaning products
- API biochemical test manual

Procedure

Part I

1. Sterilize the inoculating loop by passing it through a match flame.
2. Remove the drain plug from one sink.
3. Lower the sterile inoculating loop into the sink drain for 15 seconds.
4. Streak the wet loop onto a TSA petri dish.

Katherine Orzel was a finalist at the International Science and Engineering Fair in Fort Worth, Texas, in 1986 and continued her research on the same topic, receiving finalist honors again at the ISEF in Knoxville, Tennessee, in 1988.

5. Cover, invert, and place the petri dish in an incubator for 48 hours.

6. Wait 48 hours. Remove the petri dish from the incubator, and observe the bacterial growth.

7. Make a Gram's stain from the culture to determine whether the bacteria are gram-positive or gram-negative. This can be done by smearing a colony of bacteria from the petri dish onto a sterile glass slide. Allow the slide to dry, and then warm it by passing it over the flame of a bunsen burner.

8. Then flood the smear with crystal violet solution, and allow it to stand for 1 minute. Next, wash the smear with tap water, flood it with iodine solution, and allow it to stand for 1 minute.

9. Wash the smear again and decolorize it with 95% ethanol until the dye does not run off the smear. Wash the smear again and then counterstain it with safranine for about 30 seconds. Finally, wash it again and allow it to dry.

10. Examine the slide under the oil-immersion lens of a microscope. Gram-positive organisms will be blue, and gram-negative organisms will be red.

11. Repeat steps 1 through 10 with samples from 19 other P-traps.

Part II

1. Streak the TSA petri dishes with water cultures from 20 different P-traps in household sinks.

2. Dip sterile filter paper disks with the forceps into dilutions of the various household cleaning substances and place on the streaked petri dishes.

3. Incubate these petri dishes for 48 hours and observe the results.

4. Repeat the experiment after cleaning the P-traps with the various cleaning substances that appear to be the most effective in counteracting the bacteria.

5. Then, take more cultures from the same P-traps 18 hours later, streak them onto TSA and MacConkey petri dishes, label, and incubate them for 48 hours.

6. Observe the conditions of all the petri dishes, and make a Gram's stain (explained in steps 7 through 10 of Part I).

7. Finally, using an API manual, do an API biochemical test on the MacConkey dishes to identify the type of gram-negative bacteria present in them.

Results

1. Is the P-trap conducive for the growth of bacteria?

2. Does the type of household cleaning substance used affect the growth of the bacteria?

3. Does the length of time that the water stands in the P-trap make any difference in the bacterial growth?

4. What is the best substance to use to clean out the P-trap?

5. Were any of the bacteria found to be pathogenic?

38

The P-Trap: A Continuing Dilemma

An International Science and Engineering Fair Project

Note: This project is a continuing study of Project 37: "The P-Trap: A Bacteria Cauldron."

Purpose

The purpose of this second phase of the study is:

1. To compare water from selected P-traps that were investigated previously with samples from the same sites today.
2. To further identify organisms found in the traps.
3. To test for the presence of anaerobic bacteria.
4. To design a mechanism to control the growth of pollutant substances.

Materials Needed

- the same sinks studied in Project 37
- inoculating loop
- matches
- petri dishes: tryptic soy agar (TSA) with 5% sheep blood, and MacConkey
- Gram's stain test materials
- BBL GasPaks
- incubator
- API biochemical test manual
- reverse camp test
- dilution plate test (instructions can be found in a microbiology text)

Procedure

1. Use the sterile inoculating loop to obtain water from one of the P-traps, streak it onto a TSA petri dish, and incubate it for 48 hours. Repeat this procedure using water from the other sites.

2. Make a Gram's stain of all the petri dishes (see steps 7 through 10 in Part I of Project 37). Compare the results with the previous findings.

3. Streak two TSA petri dishes with water from one of the sites. Incubate one in a BBL GasPak and the other in a regular incubator.

4. After 48 hours, take a culture from each dish, subculture them onto separate MacConkey dishes, and incubate for 48 hours.

5. Do Gram's stain and API tests and observe.

6. Repeat Steps 3 through 5 using P-trap water from the other sites.

7. At this point, only facultative anaerobes (organisms that can be grown with or without oxygen) have been isolated from the P-trap (those incubated in the BBL GasPak). Place the TSA petri dishes into GasPaks, seal them, and leave at room temperature for 24 hours to remove the oxygen from the petri dishes.

8. Carry out four additional experiments using the same procedure as in steps 3 and 4, except that oxygen-free petri dishes should be used to isolate the anaerobic bacteria.

9. Use reverse camp tests to identify the anaerobic bacteria from the petri dishes placed in the GasPak.

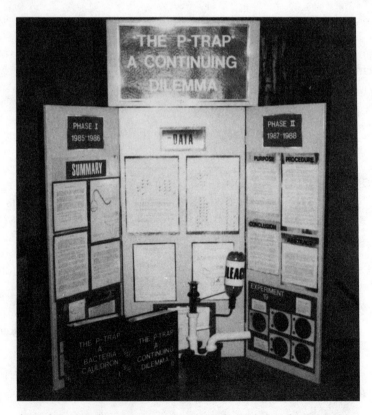

A student can always participate at another science fair with the same topic if he or she has continued research on it or expanded its objective.

10. Use the dilution plate test to determine the number of bacteria colonies, both aerobic and anaerobic, present in the P-traps.

11. Finally, review all of the experiments. Review the piping system and its impact on humans and the environment. Determine what could be done to solve this dilemma, that is, a solution to keep the P-trap bacteria-free (using what you have learned in this experiment).

Results

1. Is there any difference in the amount of bacteria now found in the P-traps with the amounts found previously?

2. How many different types of aerobic bacteria could be isolated from the P-trap?

3. Is there any correlation between the bacteria found in the P-trap and people who use the sink?

4. How long can bacteria remain dormant in the stagnant water of an unused P-trap?

5. How much bacteria, aerobic and anaerobic, was found in any given P-trap?

6. Can some type of mechanism be used in place of the P-trap, or can some device be used to keep the P-trap bacteria-free?

39

Improving the Antibacterial Effects of Garlic

An International Science and Engineering Fair Project

Purpose

To determine whether the antibacterial quality of a garlic plant can be increased by foliar applications of a garlic extract solution.

Materials Needed

- 2 garlic bulbs
- 20 plant containers
- potting soil (enough to fill 20 plant containers)
- sterile distilled water
- masking tape
- marking pen
- knife
- food processor
- cheesecloth
- 3 sterile glass containers
- 2 fine mist atomizers

- *Escherichia coli* bacteria culture
- petri dish: tryptic soy agar (TSA) with 5% sheep blood
- sterile swab
- warm tap water
- isopropyl rubbing alcohol
- dropper
- sterile filter paper disks
- sterilized forceps
- incubator
- thermometer

Experiment

Two groups of garlic plants will be grown: experimental and control. The experimental plants will have garlic extract added to their leaves by a foliar spray, while the control group will be sprayed only with water. The treated leaves will then be pulverized into a solution whose antibacterial effects will be analyzed when applied to a culture of bacteria.

Procedure

Part I

1. From one bulb of garlic obtain 20 cloves (to ensure genetic similarity), and plant one clove into each of 20 plant containers containing potting soil. Add equal amounts of sterile water to each container, watering plants as necessary.
2. Label ten plants "Experimental" and ten "Control."
3. Grow plants until leaves are present and growth is about 6 inches (15 cm) in height.

Part II—Prepare the garlic extract solution.

1. Separate the cloves from the other bulb of garlic and peel them.
2. Pulverize the cloves in the food processor until they are nearly liquefied.
3. Filter the extract by squeezing as much of the liquid portion as possible through cheesecloth into one glass container.
4. Combine one part garlic extract with one part distilled water to make up the garlic spray solution.
5. Fill one fine mist atomizer with the garlic solution. Spray each of the experimental plants with two sprays of the solution, and continue to do so every other day.
6. Fill the other fine mist atomizer with distilled water. Spray each of the control plants with two sprays of the water, and continue to do so every other day.

Part III—Prepare the culture dishes.

1. Transfer the *Escherichia coli* bacteria to the TSA petri dish with a sterile swab.
2. Mark the bottom of the plate into four equal quadrants. Label two sections "Experimental" (A and B) and two "Control" (A and B).

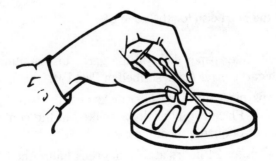

Transfer the *E. coli* bacteria to the TSA dish with a sterile swab.

Part IV—Prepare the test materials from each garlic plant.

1. Cut off the green leaves above the cloves.

2. Thoroughly wash the leaves under warm running water to remove any residue of sprayed materials.

3. Pulverize the leaves of all the experimental plants in an alcohol-sterilized food processor, filter them through cheesecloth into another container, and with the dropper, add three drops of sterile distilled water. Repeat with the control plants. (Keep the mixtures in the sterile containers until they will be used for the zone of inhibition study.)

Filter the pulverized garlic leaves through cheesecloth into the jar, and add three drops of sterile distilled water. This will be done with both the experimental and control leaves.

Part V—Prepare the petri dish for the zone of inhibition study.

1. Soak two sterile filter paper disks in the garlic test solution made from the leaves of each garlic plant (as described in Part IV).

2. With the forceps, place these two filter disks onto the two experimental quadrants of the dish. Place two filter disks soaked in the control plant mixture onto the two control quadrants of the dish.

3. Incubate the dish for 24 hours at 98.6 degrees Fahrenheit (37 degrees Celsius). Measure the diameter of the zones of inhibition in millimeters, and record your data.

Soak the sterile filter paper disks in both the experimental and control filtered leaf extracts.

Experimental A   Experimental B

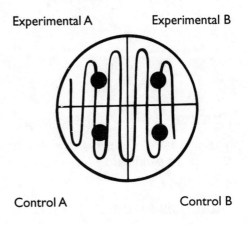

Place the two experimental filter disks onto two sections of the TSA petri dish, and place the control filter disks onto the other two sections for the zone of inhibition study.

Control A   Control B

Results

1. Compare the diameters of the zones of inhibition in the control and experimental groups. Did they differ? How much of a variance existed between the two groups? Which of the two groups had the largest diameters?

2. Which group showed the greatest antibacterial effect? Did the garlic spray affect the antibacterial quality of the garlic plant?

Does the Period of Motion of a Pendulum Depend on Its Weight, Amplitude, or Length?

Purpose

To determine if changes in the weight, amplitude, or length affect the period of motion of a pendulum.

Materials Needed

To construct the pendulum frame:

- 2-by-1-inch (5-by-2.5-cm) wood: 5 pieces 2 feet (61 cm) long for the base and top panels and 2 pieces 3 feet (0.9 meter) long for the upright sides of the frame
- 6 small metal angles and screws and/or nails

To construct the pendulum:

- screw hook
- protractor

- balance scale
- fishing weights (minimum 30 units of 1 ounce (0.028 kg) each)
- small plastic bottle with cap
- thin fishing line (minimum 10 feet (3 m))

To measure the variables:

- ruler
- kitchen balance
- stopwatch that can measure to $\frac{1}{100}$ of a second

Experiment

A simple pendulum will be constructed and set into motion several times, with changes made in its variables of weight, length, and angle of release. The average period will be computed, together with its standard deviation, for each experimental run.

Procedure

1. Assemble the pendulum frame using the diagram as a reference. Be sure to attach the screw hook to the center of the upper wood frame. Attach the protractor as shown. Weigh (W) a random number of fishing weights, put them into the small plastic bottle, and attach the cap. Cut a length (L) of the fishing line, and tie one end to the plastic bottle cap and the other to the hook. At this point the pendulum is ready to be set into motion.

2. Bring the bottle to an amplitude of (A) degrees (as indicated by the protractor) from the vertical, and release the pendulum. Time the period of motion (P) with the stopwatch. This is the time between two successive passes of the pendulum through the maximum amplitude. Repeat this procedure (N) times (e.g., ten times) to get consistent results.

3. Compute the average time period (T) and the standard deviation (S):

$$T = \Sigma P / N$$

$$S = \sqrt{\Sigma (P - T)^2 / N}$$

where $P(i = 1, 2, \ldots n)$ are the individual measured periods.

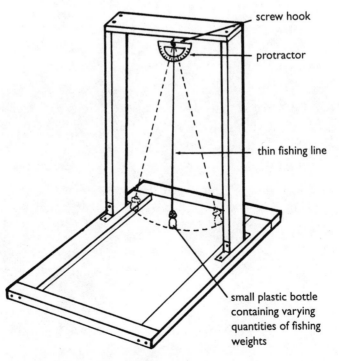

screw hook

protractor

thin fishing line

small plastic bottle containing varying quantities of fishing weights

The pendulum set in motion.

4. Repeat steps 2 and 3 with several different values for the three independent variables of length (*L*), weight (*W*), and amplitude (*A*). Select three to five different lengths, from a minimum of about 2 feet (60 cm) to the maximum allowed by the height of your pendulum. Select two or three different weights totaling from about 10 to 30 ounces (0.28 to 0.84 kg). Two or three different amplitudes can also be used in the range of 10 to 39 degrees. (Each run is, of course, characterized by the values of the three independent variables.)

Results

1. Compare the experimental results from all the trial runs with different weights. Did most of the experimental results stay close to the standard deviation (*S*) of the average period (*T*)?

2. If not, were the differences significant? Judging from your results, do you believe that the period of motion was dependent upon the weight, amplitude, or length of the pendulum?

41

Are Composites of Wood Stronger than Solid Wood?

Purpose

To determine if a wood composite, which is made of a combination of materials that have been saturated with a resin or glue, has greater torsional resistance (twisting) and drop resistance (bending) than a comparable piece of solid wood.

Materials Needed

Testing apparatus:

- 2½-by-2-feet (76-by-61-cm) panel of wood (for test platform)
- metal workshop vise with clamps (to support test bars)
- assorted screws, nuts, and bolts (to fasten the metal workshop horse to the test platform)
- round disk (calibrated in degrees) with attached 4-inch (7.6-cm) arm
- wire fishing line

- spring scale
- several ¼-pound (112-g) lead fishing weights
- ruler

Test bars:

- 10 composite bars (1 foot (30 cm) long by ⅜ inch (1 cm) square)
- 10 solid wood bars (1 foot (30 cm) long by ⅜ inch (1 cm) square)

Experiment 1: Torsional Resistance (Twisting)

Weight will be applied to the wire fishing line from the 4-inch arm at a setting of 4 pounds (1.8 kg) on the attached spring scale. This will move the arrow on the 4-inch arm to measure the degree of twist on the round disk through which the test sample passes (see diagram). This will be done to both the composite and solid test bars.

Procedure 1

1. Set up the test platform as shown in the diagram for the torsional resistance test. In general, this means that a test bar will be held between two clamps

supported by a metal workshop vise. One end of the test bar will pass through a rotating round disk that will measure the arc of twist (in degrees) on the test bar. Attached to the side of the round disk is a 4-inch arm with a hooked wire line that will suspend a spring scale. Various lead fishing weights will be hooked onto the spring scale which will cause the 4-inch arm to move downward while rotating the round disk. This will cause the test bar to twist.

2. Place the composite bar in the holding apparatus.

3. Attach the spring scale to the 4-inch arm. This will automatically place a factor of 4:1 on the scale.

4. Apply force to the wire line by adding weights to the spring scale at a predetermined weight of 4 pounds (1.8 kg). Now, measure the arc of twist on the scaled round disk.

5. Continue to increase the weight at increments of 1 pound (0.45 kg), and measure the arc of twist until the composite wood bar snaps.

6. Remove the composite bar, and repeat steps 2 through 5 with four of the composite bars and five of the solid wood bars.

Experiment 2: Drop Resistance (Bending)

The test bar will be held at one end, and a predetermined amount of weight will be applied at the opposite end, by means of an attached spring scale. The amount of drop resistance will be measured in thousandths of an inch or millimeters.

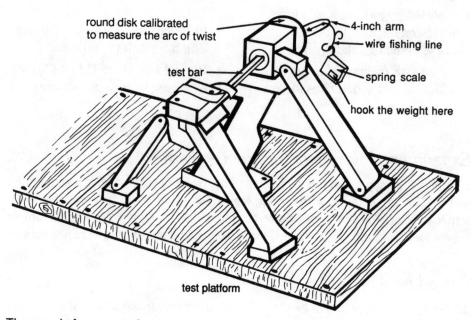

The test platform set up for the torsional resistance test.

Procedure 2

1. Set up the test platform for the drop resistance test. This can be done by removing the side of the vise with the attached round disk and 4-inch arm.
2. Place a composite bar in the remaining holding apparatus and attach the wire line to the opposite end of the bar.
3. Hook the spring scale to the wire line.
4. Apply weight through the spring scale at a predetermined weight setting, and measure the drop of the bar with a ruler.
5. Continue to increase the weight by ¼-pound (112-g) increments, and measure how far the bar drops until it snaps.
6. Remove the composite bar, and repeat steps 2 through 5 with the remaining composite bars and the remaining solid wood bars.

Results

1. Compare the amounts of weight that were needed to move each bar one degree mark when torsional resistance was tested. Which bar proved to be more resistant?
2. Compare the amounts of weight that were needed to snap each bar when drop resistance was tested. Which bar proved to be more resistant?
3. Which type of bar continued to show resistance even after the others had reached their peak resistance?
4. From your experimental results, which bar do you conclude is better at resisting force?

42

Which Angle of Attack Generates the Most Lift?

Purpose

To test four different angles of attack to determine which one generates the most lift of an airfoil.

Materials Needed

- fan
- small wind tunnel [2 feet (61 cm) in length, made of either plywood, balsa, or cardboard] (check with your science teacher for its construction)
- easel clamp
- 4 balsa airfoils of the same dimensions (each glued to the angled face of an airfoil stand)

- 4 balsa airfoil stands with 0-degree, 15-degree, 30-degree, and 50-degree angles cut into one end on each
- balsa wood testing platform
- digital metric scale
- stopwatch

Experiment

Each airfoil will be tested three times, and each test will run for 15 seconds. The 0-degree angle will serve as a control, and the other angles will act as variables. The highest force reading for each airfoil on the digital metric scale is to be recorded at the end of each test. The only variable in the experiment will be the difference in the angle of attack.

Procedure

1. Using the diagram as a general example, set up a wind tunnel testing assembly. Once the unit is set up, do not reposition the wind tunnel or testing platform. If these components are moved, the flow of air around the airfoil will change, and inaccurate results will be obtained.

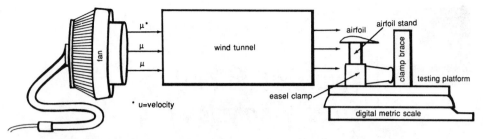

The testing assembly ready for experimentation.

2. Clamp one of the airfoils and its corresponding airfoil stand upright and place it on the balsa wood testing platform (refer to diagram). Then, place the testing assembly on the scale. The leading edge of the airfoil should be parallel to the edge of the wind tunnel's mouth.

3. Calibrate the scale.

4. Immediately after the scale has been calibrated, switch on the fan. Simultaneously, begin timing the first 15-second test with the stopwatch and record the amount of force indicated on the scale. Then repeat this procedure two more times and record the force readings.

5. Repeat steps 2 through 5 three times for each airfoil. Record the highest force reading of the three tests for each separate angle of attack.

6. Graph your results.

Results

1. From the results shown in your graphs, which angle of attack generated the most lift?

2. Why did the angles generate the particular amounts of lift force that they did?

43

Polarization and Stress Analysis of Airplane Windows

Purpose

To discover why airplane windows have an elliptical shape through a process of stress analysis called photoelasticity, and to test other possible window shapes.

Materials Needed

- 2-by-2-by-26-inch (5-by-5-by-66.5-cm) wood frame
- saw
- 6 2-inch (5-cm) squares of felt
- 2 polarizing filters
- 2 ¼-wave plates
- 2 small wooden blocks
- drill

- lamp with 200-watt light bulb (with diffusion coating)
- 35-mm-lens, single-reflex camera
- Lexon plastic (⅛-inch (0.3-cm) thick)
- glass cutter
- 2 metal rods
- 3-kg weight

Experiment

An instrument called a polariscope will be constructed to test the stresses that will occur in differently shaped model airplane windows. The shapes of the windows will be cut out of flat strips of Lexon plastic. These window models will be placed one at a time in the polariscope, while a 200-watt light bulb will shine inside from one end of the polariscope. A 3-kg weight will be loaded onto the model inside the polariscope, and dark, bright bands will appear on the stressed plastic (simulated window). These colored bands, which are called isochromatic fringes, show the stress concentration on the plastic, which represents the stresses that would be around an airplane window. The place at which the fringes are closest together is where the stress concentration is the highest.

160

Procedure

1. Build a wooden box for the frame of the polariscope (see diagram). The two ends of the box are to be left open. Cut a slot at the top and bottom of the box. Line the slot at the top of the box with felt to prevent light from going around the polarizing filters. Line the inner base of the box with felt, and leave four groove-sized gaps to support the polarizing filters and wave plates. Then, fit the two polarizing filters and wave plates into the slots. Align the two wooden blocks, and drill one hole (for a rod) through both of them. Cover the lined slot at the top of the box with the blocks. Place the lamp and the camera at opposite ends of the polariscope.

2. Cut four pieces of Lexon plastic to 1¾ inches (4.5 cm) in width and 8 inches (20.5 cm) in length. Cut out a shape in each piece with a glass cutter to represent an airplane window. Suggested shapes include: a circle, a rectangle, a diamond, and an elliptical shape (to serve as the control).

3. Drill a hole at the top and the bottom (where the metal rods will be placed) in each strip of plastic. The top rod will hold the model between the two blocks, which will allow the model to be lowered into the polariscope. The bottom rod will load the 3-kg weight onto the bottom of the model.

4. Slide one of the Lexon plastic window shapes through the top slot and insert the metal rods. Then hook on the 3-kg weight.

5. Take pictures of the isochromatic fringes, the color bands that appear near the plastic window opening on the window model inside the polariscope. Different shutter speeds can be used in case the pictures are under- or overexposed. Or you may remove the camera to look through the box end and draw the isochromatic fringes that you see.

6. Repeat steps 4 and 5 with the other window models, and record your results.

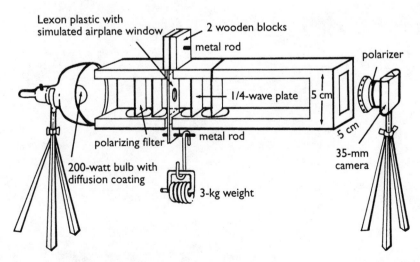

The polariscope set up for experimentation.

Results

1. Analyze the pictures of the models and their isochromatic fringes. Notice where the fringes are closest together. These areas are the points of highest stress concentration. Which areas on each model have high concentrations of stress? Which areas show the least? Why are the fringes arranged in this pattern?

2. Which models overall have less areas of high stress concentration? What explanation can be given for this?

3. Which models are the easiest to produce? Which ones are more practical and easy to use?

4. Based on your results, is the elliptical model the best shape for an airplane window? If not, which model seems to be most effective?

PHYSICS

Shape and Viscous Effect

Purpose

Spherical objects falling in viscous fluid are known to obey Stokes' Law, in the form of *drag × time = constant*. The purpose of this experiment is to determine if Stokes' Law would apply to nonspherical objects when dropped in viscous fluids, such as glycerin and corn syrup.

Materials Needed

- plastic cup
- tap water
- metric balance scale (accurate to 0.1 gram)
- 4 ounces (112 g) of glycerin
- 16 ounces (448 g) of corn syrup
- metric ruler
- metal molds (of several shapes)
- modeling clay
- lead fishing weights
- 100-ml graduated cylinder
- stopwatch (accurate to 0.01 seconds)
- 500-ml graduated cylinder

Experiment

Four sets of differently shaped clay objects (suggested are sphere, cube, teardrop, and tetrahedron), all having the same volume but different weights, will be dropped into a 100-ml graduated cylinder filled with glycerin and a 500-ml graduated cylinder filled with corn syrup. These objects will be timed with a stopwatch as each falls from the 100-ml to the 20-ml line in the glycerin and from the 500-ml to the 100-ml line in the corn syrup. Then, the buoyancy, drag, and *drag × time* for each object will be calculated. The results will be checked to see if the *drag × time* is indeed equal to that of a sphere (*constant*) which will serve as the control.

Procedure

1. Measure the density of the fluids by filling the plastic cup with water, weighing it on the balance scale, and recording the weight. Do the same with the glycerin and corn syrup. Then, divide the weight of the glycerin into the weight of the

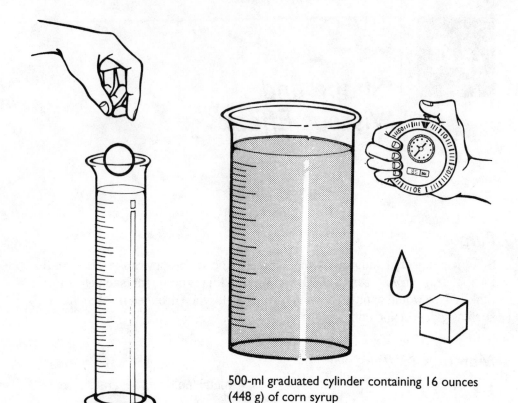

500-ml graduated cylinder containing 16 ounces (448 g) of corn syrup

100-ml graduated cylinder containing 4 ounces (112 g) of glycerin

Clay objects of various shapes will be timed as they fall through the viscous fluids to see if Stokes' Law applies to them as it does to spheres.

water to obtain the specific gravity of the glycerin. Do the same with the corn syrup.

2. Measure the volume of each metal mold. All clay objects to be made in the same mold will have the same volume.

3. Press clay into the molds. Be sure that the molds are completely filled with the clay.

4. To make clay objects of varying weights, force one or two lead fishing weights in the molds. Scrape off all excess clay (to maintain the same volume). Make an equal number of objects with different weights, but of the same volume, for each shape.

5. Test: Drop one of the spheres into the 100-ml graduated cylinder of glycerin, and start the stopwatch as soon as it hits the 100-ml line. Watch carefully as it glides through the glycerin. The moment it hits the 20-ml line, stop the stopwatch and record the time. Calculate the buoyancy, drag, and *drag × time* as the constant. The buoyancy is the object's volume (submerged in the fluid) multiplied by the fluid density. The weight of the object minus the buoyancy is

the drag. Repeat for each object in the glycerin and then in the 500-ml graduated cylinder of corn syrup to compare the times for each, and to see if Stokes' Law applies to the differently shaped objects.

Results

1. What was the time "constant" of the spheres dropped in glycerin?

2. How did the times of the cubes, teardrops, and tetrahedrons compare with those of the spheres?

3. From your observations, would you say that Stokes' Law applied to any of the differently shaped objects?

What Would Happen to Climate, Weather Patterns, and Life Forms if the Earth Were Cubical?

Purpose

To theorize what effects a cube-shaped earth would have on climate, weather patterns, and flora/fauna life.

Materials Needed

Experiment 1

- 2 empty half-gallon milk cartons
- knife or scissors
- baking soda
- water
- white paper
- tape or glue
- world map
- pencil
- metric ruler
- transparency film marker
- sheet of transparency film
- overhead projector
- globe

Experiment 2

- hollow plastic ball [approx. 5-inch (12-cm) diameter]
- sharp knife
- empty half-gallon milk carton
- 2 unsharpened pencils with erasers
- 2 thumb tacks
- modeling clay
- small squeeze bottle
- water
- food coloring
- a helper

Experiment 1

A grid will be drawn on a sheet of transparency film and projected onto an upright parallel globe to simulate the sun and to measure the concentrations of sunlight on various points of a spherical earth. The same will be done with a cubical earth, and the results of each will be compared.

Procedure 1

1. Construct a cubical model of the earth by cutting off the bottoms of two empty half-gallon milk containers and fitting them together. (The milk odor can be removed by soaking the cartons in a solution of baking soda and water for about 15 minutes.) Then, tape or glue the white paper to the cube. Refer to the world map and draw the continents and oceans onto the cube as you think they might appear.

2. Use the metric ruler and the transparency film marker to make a grid on the clear sheet of transparency film, with each square measuring 1 cc. Next, place the grid onto the overhead projector and beam the grid image onto an upright globe that is positioned parallel with the projector.

3. Locate a grid square beaming directly at a place near the 45-degree latitude mark on the globe. Outline the shape directly on the globe. Repeat this procedure, locating a grid shape directly below the first, but at a place near the equator. Measure the length and width of each outlined shape, calculate its area, and note the concentration of light in each. This will simulate the angles at which sunlight strikes the earth's spherical surface and the amount of light concentration at each angle.

4. Repeat step 3 using the cubical earth. For the 45-degree mark, measure one-fourth of the distance into the center of the light-exposed side. For the equator, measure halfway into the center of the light-exposed side.

Results 1

Compare the grid areas of the spherical earth to those of the cubical earth. Were there any differences in the way the simulated sunlight was concentrated on the different outlined points? If so, what do you think the overall climate of the cubical earth would be like?

Experiment 2

Cut a half-sphere out of a hollow plastic ball and a half-cube out of the bottom of a half-gallon milk container. Each will be tacked loosely to the eraser tops of two pencils so that they may spin freely. Then, each pencil unit will stand straight up in a lump of modeling clay. As the half-sphere and half-cube are spun, a steady stream of liquid will be squeezed over their surface. This procedure will theoretically compare and contrast weather systems between a spherical earth and a cubical earth.

Procedure 2

1. Cut the ball in half. Then cut out a cube from the bottom of the empty milk container. Tack the centers of each loosely to the eraser tops of two pencils. Stand each pencil unit straight up in its own lump of clay with the eraser end up. Test the half-sphere and cube to be sure that they spin freely without sliding down.

2. Fill the squeeze bottle half full with the mixture of water and food coloring. Then, spin the half-sphere while your helper squirts a steady stream of the colored dye on the half-sphere. Note the pattern made by the dye as it travels off the half-sphere.

3. Repeat step 2 with the half-cube.

Results 2

1. Compare and contrast the concentration of light between the same continent and ocean locations on the spherical earth and the cubical earth.

2. Was there any difference in the dye patterns between the two models?

3. What kind of effects would the angle at which the sunlight strikes a cubical earth, and the way weather systems move across a cubical earth have on its flora and fauna?

PHYSICS

46

The Physics of Cheating in Baseball

Purpose

To determine whether cork, sawdust, or rubber balls, when illegally used as fillers in hollowed-out wooden baseball bats, will cause a baseball to travel farther and give it greater speed upon impact, compared to a heavier, solid wooden bat.

Materials Needed

- 4 solid wooden bats (same length and weight)
- vise
- workbench
- safety goggles
- drill
- rolled cork
- sawdust
- rubber balls (1 inch (2.5 cm) in diameter)
- scale
- wood putty
- sandpaper
- batting device (can be constructed with: screws, eye

bolts, nuts, a spring, a hinge, two metal straps, 1 2-by-10-by-40-inch (5-by-25-by-100-cm) board, and 1 2-by-6-by-26-inch (5-by-15-by-65-cm) board)
- baseball
- batting tee
- screwdriver
- tape measure
- radar gun to track speed of baseball (may be obtained by permission of local police department)
- an adult helper
- helpers to bat

Experiment

Three hollow wooden baseball bats, one filled with rolled cork, one with sawdust, and one with rubber balls, and one solid wooden bat will be attached to a batting device in turn. Each bat will spring from the batting device and hit the baseball, which will be set on a tee. The distance at which the ball travels as well as its

169

speed when hit by each bat will be measured and recorded to determine which bat has the greatest effect on the baseball.

Procedure

Part I—Prepare the bats.

1. With adult supervision, safety goggles, and the vise, drill through the tip of one solid wooden bat and hollow out a chamber that is 1 inch (2.5 cm) wide in diameter and 8 inches (20 cm) deep. Repeat this procedure for two additional bats.

2. Fill the chamber of the first bat with rolled cork, the second with sawdust, and the third with rubber balls. Weigh each of the filled bats to ensure that they are lighter than the solid wooden bat. Seal the tips of the bats with wood putty. When dry, smooth the tips with sandpaper and weigh each bat again.

Part II—Build the batting device.

1. Attach the end of the smaller board to the top of the larger board with a hinge so that the boards are perpendicular to each other, as shown in the diagram.

2. Connect the coiled spring between the two boards (as shown in the diagram) and fasten with eye bolts. Be sure that the spring is coiled enough so that when the horizontal board is pulled back and released, it will spring forward.

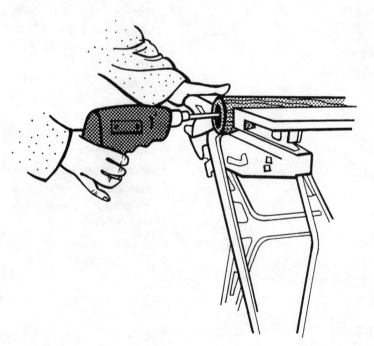

Under the supervision of an adult, drill through the tips of three wooden baseball bats to hollow chambers that are 1 inch (2.5 cm) wide in diameter and 8 inches (20 cm) deep.

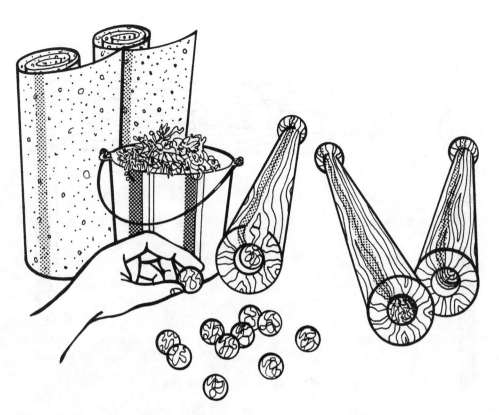

Fill the chamber of each hollowed-out bat with cork, sawdust, and rubber balls, respectively.

3. Screw two metal straps to the horizontal board in such a manner that they will support and hold the handle of a baseball bat.

Part III—Test for distance.

1. Transport your batting device, batting tee, bats, and baseball to an open outdoor area such as a playing field or park and secure the vertical board into the ground. Unscrew the metal straps on the batting device to attach one of the bats, and reattach the straps to secure the bat in position. Adjust the height and position of the batting device so that the bat will be parallel to the top of the batting tee. Place the baseball on the batting tee, and pull the horizontal board of the batting device back 180 degrees from its resting position and release. Note the exact location where the ball first bounces, and measure the distance from the batting tee to this location. Record your results. Repeat this procedure 25 times for each bat in the batting device at the same angle and tension, to ensure the accuracy of your data.

2. Repeat the test for distance by replacing the batting device with human subjects. Have each batter hit the baseball off the tee a total of ten times with each bat, and measure the distance between the tee and the first bounce. Record your results.

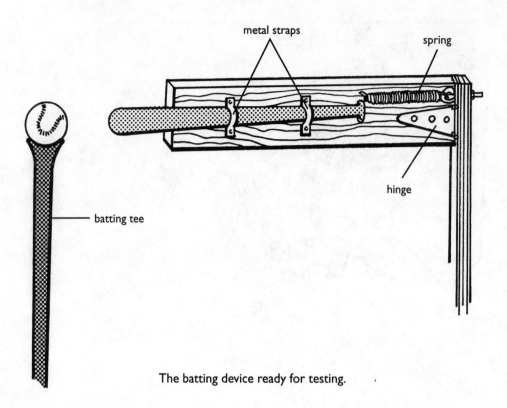

metal straps

spring

batting tee

hinge

The batting device ready for testing.

Part IV—Test for speed.

1. If a radar gun can be obtained, set it up to measure the speed at which the ball travels after being hit by the filled bats and the solid wooden bat. Repeat this procedure 25 times with each bat in the batting device at the same angle and tension, to ensure the accuracy of your data.

2. Repeat the test for speed by replacing the batting device with human subjects. Again, have each batter hit the baseball a total of ten times with each bat, and measure the speed at which the balls travel after being hit from the filled bats and the solid wooden bat.

Results

1. Which baseball bat made the baseball travel the farthest when placed in the batting device? Which baseball bat made the baseball travel the fastest when placed in the batting device? Which variables may have accounted for these results; i.e., was it the weight or the composition of the bat?

2. Did the results of your distance or speed tests vary when human variables were added? If so, in what way?

PHYSICS

47

Does a Golf Ball's Bounciness Influence the Distance that It Will Travel?

Purpose

To determine whether the ability of a golf ball to bounce has any relationship to the distance it travels when hit by a golf club.

Materials Needed

- 24 golf balls (3 each of 8 different brands)
- marking pen
- tape measure
- screwdriver
- screws
- 3 2-by-4-inch (5-by-10-cm) wood sections
- saw (use with an adult's help)
- 36-by-36-inch (90-by-90-cm) plywood section that is ¾ inch thick
- 2 eye-lag bolts
- sheet rock screws
- 2 ¾-inch (1.9-cm) plywood sections for corner hinge support and club support
- metal door hinge
- 4-iron gold club head with shortened shaft
- metal door spring ¾ inch (1.9 cm) in diameter and 6 inches (15 cm) in length
- golf tees
- an adult
- a helper

Experiment

A number of golf balls will be tested to determine the height of their bounce when dropped on a hard surface from a set height. Then, the same balls will be hit with the striking mechanism, and the distance to the first bounce of each ball will be measured to determine if the ball that bounces the highest is the one that travels the farthest.

Procedure

Part I—Conduct the bounce test.

1. Group all golf balls by brand name and number each with a marking pen.

2. Select a reference height over a hard surface. A good location would be a brick or cement wall that runs along a cemented or paved surface. Secure the tape measure at the base of the wall and tape it vertically.

3. Have your helper sit on top of the wall, place a golf ball on the edge, and roll it until it drops onto the hard surface. Measure the height of the first bounce against your measuring tape and record your reading. Repeat this step five times with the same ball as well as with different balls of the same brand. Average the bounce heights to obtain a single value for the brand name. Repeat until all of the golf balls have been tested.

Part II—Build the golf ball striking mechanism.

1. Screw one of the 2-by-4-inch wood sections perpendicular to the tops of the other two to form the mechanism's frame. With the adult's help, saw the large plywood section into three parts to form the base and side panels for the mechanism (see diagram).

2. From one of the ¾-inch plywood sections, cut a corner hinge support and attach it to the upper left corner of the mechanism, as shown in the diagram. From the other ¾-inch plywood section, cut a section for mounting the golf club, as shown in the diagram. Attach the door hinge to the club mount section, and secure the 4-iron club head with the shortened shaft. Attach this unit to the corner hinge support, and connect the door spring (see diagram).

3. Position the springed club in its resting position, and align it with a golf tee set on the base.

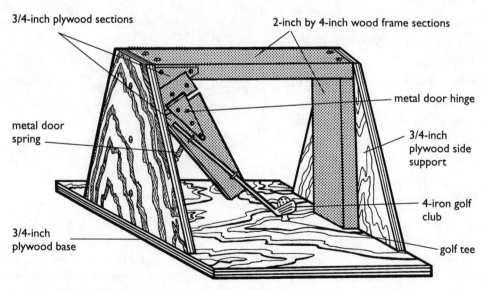

3/4-inch plywood sections

2-inch by 4-inch wood frame sections

metal door hinge

metal door spring

3/4-inch plywood side support

4-iron golf club

3/4-inch plywood base

golf tee

The golf ball striking mechanism ready for testing.

Part III—Conduct the distance test.

1. Transport the golf ball striking mechanism to an open outdoor area such as a playing field or park. Firmly anchor the mechanism to the ground if possible.

2. Place one of the golf balls on the golf tee inside the mechanism, and pull the club unit back to its maximum position and release. Note the exact location where the ball first lands, and measure the distance it traveled. Repeat this step five times with the same ball as well as with different balls of the same brand. Average the distances to obtain a single value for the brand name. Repeat until all of the golf balls have been tested.

Results

1. Did all of the golf balls of the same brand have the same bounce heights? If not, what variables may have accounted for different results?

2. Did all of the golf balls of the same brand travel the same distance? If not, what variables may have accounted for different results?

3. How did all of the brands compare in the bounce test? In the distance test? Does there appear to be a difference in the construction of each golf ball?

4. Which ball bounced the highest? Traveled the farthest? Did the ball that bounced the highest travel the farthest?

48

Relaxing the Breathing Patterns of Newly Purchased Pet Fish So They May Adapt to a New Aquarium

Note: The International Science and Engineering Fair has established strict guidelines to which all of its affiliate fairs must adhere. These guidelines involve experimentation with vertebrate animals. It is the responsibility of the student to follow these rules carefully. (See the Foreword and/or contact Science Service, the administrator of the ISEF, for a copy of the applicable rules.)

Purpose

Because of the drastic environmental changes that occur as a fish moves from a pet shop aquarium, to a plastic bag, to a home aquarium, the immune systems of many pet fish become weakened. Fish tanks are usually filled with tap water that is "bubbly" with oxygen gas. The fish often become sick from the shock and the high amount of undissolved oxygen in their bloodstreams. This experiment will determine if calcium carbonate (a compound that reduces excess gas), when applied to either fish food or fish tank water, has any effect in dissolving the amount of oxygen gas present in the fishes' bodies so that the fish may relax and adapt to their new homes more easily.

Materials Needed

- 3 fish tanks (1 gallon (3.8 liters) each)
- fresh tap water
- 3 fish from a pet shop (of the same breed)
- ½ teaspoon (2.5 ml) of calcium carbonate
- pet fish food (for example, Tetramin brand)
- mortar and pestle

Experiment

One fish will be placed into a tank already containing the calcium carbonate, while another fish will be placed in a different tank and receive the calcium carbonate in its food (experimental groups). A third fish will remain in a tank filled with fresh tap water and plain fish food (control). The fishes will be monitored closely to count their number of gill movements per minute and their level of activity.

Procedure

1. Fill each fish tank with an equal amount of fresh tap water. Then, place all three newly purchased pet shop fish into one of the tanks. For the first minute, record the rate at which their gills move and their levels of activity.

2. Stir ¼ teaspoon (1.25 ml) of calcium carbonate into the second tank. After it has dissolved into the water, place one of the fish into the tank and sprinkle in some plain fish food. Record the fish's gill movements, activity, and appetite.

3. Place a different fish into the third tank. Prepare this fish's food by powdering a serving size of fish food with a mortar and pestle. Then mix ¼ teaspoon (1.25 ml) of calcium carbonate and several drops of water into the powdered food. Mix into the fish tank. Record the gill movements, level of activity, and appetite of this fish.

4. Allow the remaining fish to stay in the original tank. Feed it a meal of plain fish food only. Again, observe its gill movements, activity level, and appetite.

5. Continue to monitor all the fish constantly for the first hour, or until each fish has completely adapted to its environment.

Results

1. How did the fish react when they were originally placed together in the tap water tank? Did they appear different from the way they looked in the pet store? What were the number of gill movements per minute?

2. Did the calcium carbonate appear to have any effect in aiding the fish to adapt to their new environment? If so, which method of administering the compound appeared to be the best?

3. Which fish appeared to have adapted to its environment most quickly? What were its gill movements per minute after it had appeared to relax?

ZOOLOGY

49

Can the Heartbeat of a Chicken Embryo Be Detected Without Breaking Its Eggshell?

Note: It is recommended that this experiment be conducted under the supervision of a research scientist. The International Science and Engineering Fair has established strict guidelines to which all of its affiliate fairs must adhere. These guidelines involve experimentation with vertebrate animals. It is the responsibility of the student to follow those rules carefully. (See the Foreword and/or contact Science Service, the administrator of the ISEF, for a copy of the applicable rules.)

Purpose

To see if it is possible to measure the early heartbeat of a chicken embryo without breaking its eggshell or disturbing the chick's development—as other methods have done in the past.

Materials Needed

- Zygo Axiom 200 interferometer
- retroreflector and mount
- VAX computer by Digital Equipment Co.
- 3 3-day-old incubated fertile chicken eggs
- 1 3-day-old dead chicken egg
- incubator

Experiment

The movement within an eggshell will be measured with a Zygo Axiom 200 interferometer (which sends a light from a laser through a beam splitter that splits the light beam in half). One half of that light will travel out to a fixed mirror and bounce back. The other half will travel out to a movable mirror that is touching an egg, so that when its eggshell moves from the embryo's heartbeat, the mirror will also move. Therefore, the beam that will bounce off the movable mirror will have its phase altered in such a way that when it returns to the beam splitter (where it is combined with the other beam), constructive interference will result from the action of the waves joining in phases. Destructive interference will occur if the waves are out of phase. Then, the changes in the distance traveled by the beam going to the egg (in millionths of a millimeter) will be calculated from the patterns of light intensity. The experiment will be repeated on two more fertile embryos (to achieve consistent results) and on a dead embryo (as a control).

Procedure

1. Obtain permission to work under the supervision of a research scientist, probably at a local university.
2. Set up the Zygo Axiom 200 interferometer and the retroreflector and mount with your supervisor's assistance, and connect the apparatus to a VAX computer that will record the data of the changing phases of the beam.

Celeste Peterson found that the interferometer technique was extremely sensitive in picking up the tiny shell vibrations from the 3-day-old chicken embryos without breaking the chicks' eggshells or disturbing their progress.

3. Obtain three fertile chicken eggs, together with a dead one (to serve as the control), all of which are about 3 days old. Store them in an incubator. Place one egg at a time gently up against the movable mirror on the retroreflector, and expose it to the light beam for 1½ minutes to collect shell vibrations as data points. Repeat the procedure again when the eggs are 4 and 5 days old.

4. After the data points of the heartbeat frequencies have been sent to the VAX computer, they will be put onto a graph and analyzed as time versus displacement.

5. After experimentation, observe the condition of the eggshells for cracks, and carefully observe the eggs until they hatch, to see if this method has disturbed the chicks' progress in any way.

Results

1. According to your recorded data, what were the average beats per second in each embryo?

2. Were the beats per second less detectable as the embryo matured? Why do you suppose this occurred?

3. Did any of the eggshells crack as a result of experimentation? How long did it take before the eggs hatched? Were the chicks underdeveloped or harmed?

4. What other applications could this method have in studying the development of embryos inside shells?

ZOOLOGY

50

Are Dogs Colorblind?

Note: The International Science and Engineering Fair has established strict guidelines to which all of its affiliate fairs must adhere. These guidelines involve experimentation with vertebrate animals. It is the responsibility of the student to follow those rules carefully. (See the Foreword and/or contact Science Service, the administrator of the ISEF, for a copy of the applicable rules.)

Purpose

To determine if dogs are in fact completely colorblind, as many people believe.

Materials Needed

- assorted colored construction paper
- camera
- black and white film
- 3 glass jars
- 1 dog—any age, breed, or sex, in good health
- dog biscuits or some other treat the dog likes

Experiment

Photographs of colored construction paper will be taken with black and white film to determine how colors appear under varying amounts of light. These pictures will simulate how shades of color would be perceived by a totally colorblind dog. A dog will be trained to consistently choose a jar covered with paper of one shade (as it appears from the photos) from a distinctly differently shaded jar. Once the dog is trained to choose the particular jar, the other jar will be replaced by a jar of a different shade but with similar contrast to the one the dog is trained to choose. The jar positions will be switched frequently to determine whether the dog can still recognize the shaded jar that it was trained to choose.

Procedure

1. Take black and white photographs of an assortment of colored construction paper to determine which colors appear to have similar and dissimilar degrees of brightness and contrast after the film is developed.

After the dog has been trained to choose one jar of a particular degree of brightness and contrast over a distinctly differently shaded jar, color vision will then be necessary when the dog must choose the same jar as opposed to another one with a similar degree of brightness and contrast.

2. Cover two jars with differently colored construction paper that share a similar contrast and brightness when photographed with black and white film. Cover the third jar with another color whose photographed shade is distinctly different from the other two.

3. For the first part of your experiment, the dog will not be tested for colorblindness but will be trained to select one of two similarly shaded jars from the differently shaded one. When the dog can consistently choose the correct jar, reward it with a treat.

4. For the second part of your experiment, replace the jar that the dog was not trained to choose with the second similarly shaded jar. The dog will need color vision to distinguish between the two jars, since with complete colorblindness the two colors would appear to be the same brightness and contrast.

5. Switch the positions of the jars around frequently, and test the dog 100 times. If the dog chooses correctly, continue to reward it to keep it interested. Chart the number of correct and incorrect responses made by the dog in the second part of your experiment.

Results

1. Was the dog able to distinguish between degrees of brightness and contrast in the first part of your experiment?

2. Was the dog consistently correct, incorrect, or did it vary in its responses?

3. Was the dog able to distinguish between the similar shades in the second part of your experiment?

4. Was the dog consistently correct, incorrect, or did it vary in its responses?

5. If the dog was mostly correct, do you think that other variables may have accounted for its accuracy?

PART

III

Appendixes

APPENDIX A

400 IDEAS FOR SCIENCE FAIR PROJECT TOPICS

The following is a listing of sample science fair project ideas from various scientific fields that can be used to focus on a possible project topic.

A

Acoustics

comparison of acoustic models

study of anechoic chambers

study of the acoustics of music

methods of noise control

sound holography

analysis of sound waves

comparison of materials used for sound amplification

Aerodynamics

drag study

analysis of, in vehicles

effect of wind design on velocity and distance

correlation between wheel diameter and speed

effects of turbulence

wind tunnel design

Agriculture

study of irrigation methods

comparison of soil types

analysis of various feeds

analysis of chemicals used in farming

effect of fertilizers on plant and animal life

soil chemistry and composition

analysis of pesticides used in farming

Air

effects of smog

effects of aerosols

study of airborne infections

study of air quality in various buildings

Alcohol

as a fuel

physiological effects of

Amino Acids

metabolism of, in the body

interaction of, in the body

method for determining human body absorption rates

Anesthesia

side effects of

comparison of effects between individuals

alternative anesthetics

Animals

communication between

learning in/training of

environmental effects on animal migration

environmental effects on animal behavior

Antibiotics

comparison of effectiveness between types

sources of

analysis of allergic reactions to

Aquaculture

study of algae cultures

scientific techniques for fisheries

effects of water temperature and salinity level on fish hatching

Arteries

calcification of

prevention of disease in

methods for improving arterial circulation

Astronomy

analysis of satellite designs

study of the moon's effects on nature

effects of sunspots on weather systems

predicting the positioning of an object in orbit

Automobiles

modifications of and improvements in

analysis of safety devices for

identification and effects of vehicle emissions

B

Batteries

effects of storage temperatures on

methods for running AC devices on DC power

Behavior

behavior modification of children through reinforcement techniques

correlations between IQ and memory

effects of classical music on learning

effects of television on social development of children

effects of birth order on social development

Blood

chemistry and composition of

diseases of

clotting time of

variations in blood cell counts

effects on platelet aggregation

regeneration of bone marrow

Bones

chemistry and composition of

abnormalities in

analysis of fracture types

diseases of

absorption of calcium supplements by

Botany

plant breeding analysis

plant cloning techniques

medicinal uses of plants

external effects on plant growth

nutrient deficiencies in hydroponically grown plants

effects of hormones on plant tissue cultures

effects of soil erosion on plants

methods for treating Crown Gall disease

biochemical changes in plants in various environments

Brain

methods for diagnosing Alzheimer's disease

effects of physical injury on

correlation between memory and nucleic acid

Building and Construction

bridge engineering

study of strains and stresses

comparison of strengths of building materials

comparison of insulation materials

effects of weather upon structures

fire preventative building materials

C

Cells

effects on division of

effects on function of

effects of ultraviolet radiation on

Chemistry

comparison of chemical bonds

effects of chemical reactions

effects of chemical toxins in the environment

methods for absorbing wastewater metallic ions

Children

learning disabilities in

sleeping needs of

methods for modifying behavior

study of growth and development in children

study of childhood diseases

Cigarettes

collection efficiency of cigarette filters

physiological effects of direct smoking compared to indirect smoking

Color

perception of

effects of, on plant growth

physiological effects of

psychological effects of

Computers

program designs for

robotic applications for

physiological effects of computer screens

Corrosion

study of chemical changes in

methods for prevention of

role of microbes in

Crystals

factors affecting the growth of

mathematical patterns found in

applications of chemical crystallography

magnetic properties of

comparison of structures between various types

D

Dairy Studies

microbial action in dairy products

comparison of cow feeds

effects of dairy products in digestion

treatment of viruses in dairy cattle

E

Environmental Studies

handling and transportation of toxic wastes

landfills and groundwater contamination

analysis of a closed ecological system

neutralization of toxic wastes

effects of pollutants on wildlife

Erosion

methods for controlling

effects of weather in

effects on soil composition

Eye

study of diseases in

study of abnormalities in

effects of various vitamin supplements on

effects of ultraviolet radiation upon

effects of age on peripheral vision

color and light sensitivity of

perception of optical illusions among age groups

F

Fermentation

study of chemical changes in

identification and role of microbes in

analysis of enzymatic stimulation

Fertilizers

chemistry and composition of

effects of on the environment

comparison and evaluation of various types

comparison of organic and inorganic

Fish

effects of contaminated water upon

medicinal uses of fish oils

study of diseases found in

comparison of different species

migration patterns of

Food

methods of treating contamination of

physiological effects of additives used for preservation

comparison of nutritional contents of

body absorption of nutrients from

effects of packaging upon

food-dwelling microbes

dehydration and preservation of

analysis and comparison of radiated food quality

allergic reactions to

effects of pesticides on food quality

Fungi

environmental effects of mold spores

medicinal uses of

practical applications of, for industry

means of preventing the growth of

G

Gasoline

chemistry and composition of

comparison of efficiency of various octane levels

analysis of the byproducts from

Genetics

study of genetic diseases

methods for transferring genes

Geology

study of the geologic history of an area

relationship between the moon and earthquake activity

Glucose

metabolism in the body

study of sugar inversion

H

Hair

physiological effects of hair dyes and chemicals

hair transplanting

effects of disease on

effects of diet on

Health

analysis of various diets

effects of climate on

side effects of medications

analysis of various exercises

Heart

external effects on blood pressure and pulse rate

abnormalities in

effects of diet on

study of diseases found in

Heat

therapeutic uses of

insulation for retaining heat

analysis of efficiency of various heating mechanisms

Hydraulics

pumping design modifications

analysis of turbines

methods for irrigation improvement

I

Ice

comparison of various ice melters

effects of, on microbes

effects of, on bodily tissues

therapeutic and surgical uses of

Immune System

methods of vaccination

in vitro immunization of cells

study of disorders affecting

study of biochemical processes in

Infants

chemistry and content of baby food/
    formula

study of growth and behavior of

presence of hand dexterity and
    preference in

Infrared Rays

image converters

industrial applications of

therapeutic uses of

effects of, on heating

effects of, on the environment

Insects

study of behavior and communication
    in

parasitic effects of

methods for extermination of

methods for sterilization of

comparison of species in different
    locations

diseases carried by

L

Lasers

use of, in communications

use of, in surgery

effects of, upon the environment

Lead

methods for detection of

physiological effects of ingestion of

Learning

influence of gender in

memory, reasoning, and spatial
    abilities between age groups

study of learning disabilities

methods for subliminal learning

effects of diet on

Light

influence of, in chemical reactions

psychological and physiological effects of

therapeutic uses of

applications of, in photography

Lipids

amounts needed in diet

metabolism of, in various animals

cholesterol factor tests

Liquids

viscosity comparisons

effects of, upon acoustics

Lungs

environmental effects upon

study of diseases found in

effects of nutrition on

M

Magnetics

effects of magnetic fields

industrial applications of magnets

Marine Engineering

ship propulsion methods

sea pollution control

Mathematics

correlation between number systems

studies in probability

analysis of various functions

mathematical patterning in nature

Metabolism

effects of dieting on

effects of diet pills on

variation of, among animals

chemical factors affecting

Metals

corrosion inhibitors

refining processes

oxidation rate comparisons

variations in the atomic densities of

Meteorology

methods for forecasting

analysis of weather patterns

comparison of rainfall between locations

artificial effects upon weather

Minerals

medicinal uses of

as nutritional supplements

contents found in various soil samples

contents found in various water samples

O

Ocean

ocean waves as an energy source

effects of pollution on

methods for biodegrading oil spills

Oil

refining modifications

effects of, on the environment

nontraditional applications in industry

Orthopedics

prosthetic device designs

artificial joint designs

study of therapeutic exercises

Oxygen

effects of, in chemical reactions

therapeutic uses of

industrial application of

methods for air purification

P

Parasites

prevention of parasitic microbes

study of parasitic diseases

methods for extermination of

Perception

comparison of visual perception
between children and adults

study of disorders affecting

methods for learning through

Pesticides

effects of, on the environment

storage containers for

biodegradation of

Photography

lens modifications

effects of temperature upon film and
development

methods for surgical use of

uses of laser photography

Plastics

effects of, on the environment

surgical applications of

effects of radiation on

Pollution

chemistry and composition of various
water and soil samples

methods for controlling

analysis of purification mechanisms

analysis of sewage disposal
mechanisms

Ponds, Lakes, Rivers

current power as an energy source

analysis of water quality among
locations

analysis of seasonal changes in, on
wildlife

comparison of dissolved oxygen rates
among locations

chemistry and composition of water
samples

Proteins

nutritional importance of

metabolism of, in various animals

lipoprotein patterns in various age
groups

R

Radiation

physiological effects of

methods of protection against

uses of, in food preservation

uses of, in sterilization

Radiography

uses of, in medicine

physiological side effects of

industrial applications of

Radios

comparison of power supplies for

radio frequency uses

methods of eliminating radio
interference

methods of improving sound in

Rain

chemistry and composition of
raindrops

comparison of rainfall patterns among
locations

study of rain erosion

Recycling

methods for recycling plastic

effects of, on the internal bonding of
paper

comparison of recycling techniques

methods of developing a waste
management system

Reservoirs

methods of sediment control in

methods of water purification in

S

Saline Water Conversion

study of distillation processes

methods of electrodialysis

Salt

use of, as a fertilizer

antibacterial effects of

physiological effects of

Seawater

chemistry and composition of

study of corrosion by

study of microbes from various ocean
locations

effects of environment on

Seeds

germination techniques

study of diseases in

effects of radiation on

Sewage

chemistry and composition of

use of, as a fertilizer

methods for the purification of

study of the biodegradation of

as an energy resource

Silicon

surgical uses of

biodegradability of

Skin

effects of medication on

effects of ultraviolet radiation on

methods of protecting and improving
quality of

methods of skin grafting

study of diseases found in

Sleep

physiological needs for in children and
adults

study of sleeping disorders

observation of various stages of

effects of, on behavior

influence of, on circadian rhythms

effects of sleep deprivation on
concentration

Soil

chemistry and composition of

methods of conservation of

methods of controlling erosion of

Sun

measure of radiation from, at various
locations and times

evaluation of lotions with various sun
protection factors

medicinal effects of

comparison of solar energy with other
sources

Surgery

analysis of surgical techniques

biodegradability of prosthetic
implants

side effects of anesthesia

T

Telescopes

study of various lenses

use of mathematics in

modifications of

factors affecting resolution powers in

Tobacco

chemistry and composition of

diseases caused by

use of, as a fertilizer

analysis of substitutes for

U

Ultraviolet Rays

effects of, on plants/animals

use of, for water purification

therapeutic uses of

V

Vaccinations

methods of inoculating

serum sources

physiological side effects of

Vitamins

study of metabolism of, in the human body

study of deficiencies of

therapeutic uses of

study of interaction of

W

Water

chemistry and composition of

methods of purification of

effects of pollution on

analysis of water quality between various locations

comparison of pH levels between various locations

study of filtration methods

Wildlife

methods of conservation of

prevention of disease in

methods of improving habitats of

Wind

effects of, on soil erosion

use of, as an energy source

comparison of windmill designs

study of wind turbines

Wood

chemistry and composition of

microbes found in

fireproofing techniques

use of, as an energy source

X

X rays

physiological effects of

safety devices for use with

alternative industrial uses for

Y

Yeast

chemistry and composition of

uses of, in fermentation

physiological effects of

industrial uses of

APPENDIX B

U.S. SCIENTIFIC SUPPLY COMPANIES

The following is a listing of 41 scientific supply companies from whom laboratory materials and other scientific supplies and instruments can be obtained. The companies were selected because they specialize in equipment geared to science fair projects or equipment that is normally used in a school laboratory.

EAST

Baylis-American Co., Inc.
365 Charles St.
Providence, RI 02940
(401) 421-0828

Bowman-Mell & Co., Inc.
1334 Howard St.
Harrisburg, PA 17105
(717) 238-5235

Burrell Corp.
2223 Fifth Ave.
Pittsburgh, PA 15219
(412) 471-2527

Connecticut Valley Biological Supply Co.
82 Valley Rd.
Southampton, MA 01703
(413) 527-4030
(800) 628-7748

Edmund Scientific Co.
101 E. Gloucester Pike
Barrington, NJ 08007
(609) 547-8880

Learning Ideas, Inc.
5570 Silver Hill Rd.
District Heights, MD 20747
(301) 420-9211

Learning Things, Inc.
P.O. Box 436
Arlington, MA 02174
(617) 646-0093

Science Fair by ISSC
College Square Shopping Center
Newark, DE 19711
(302) 453-1817

Science Kit and Boreal Labs
777 E. Park Dr.
Tonawanda, NY 14150
(716) 874-6020
(800) 828-7777

Thomas Scientific
99 High Hill Rd.
P.O. Box 99
Swedesboro, NJ 08085
(609) 467-2000

Ward's Natural Science Establishment,
    Inc.
5100 W. Henrietta Rd.
Rochester, NY 14586
(800) 962-2660

World of Science
Corporate Headquarters
Rochester, NY 14623
(716) 475-0100

SOUTHEAST

Advance Scientific & Chemical, Inc.
2345 S.W. 34th St., Suite 3
Fort Lauderdale, FL 33312
(800) 524-2436

Carolina Biological Supply Co.
2700 York Rd.
Burlington, NC 27215
(910) 584-0381
(800) 334-5551

Kenin Scientific Preferred
1830 N.E. 163 St.
North Miami Beach, FL 33162
(305) 949-7681

Rowlab Scientific
1650 Art Museum Dr.
Jacksonville, FL 32207
(904) 399-8036

Science Hobbies, Inc.
2615 Central Ave.
Charlotte, NC 28205
(704) 375-7684

CENTRAL

American Science & Surplus
5696 N. Northwest Hwy.
Chicago, IL 60646
(312) 763-0313

American Science & Surplus
1631 W. Oklahoma Ave.
Milwaukee, WI 53219
(414) 541-7777

BME Lab Store
2459 University Ave., W.
St. Paul, MN 55114
(612) 646-5339

Bryan Biological, Inc.
17800 E. Warren
Detroit, MI 48224
(313) 886-7404

Capitol Scientific, Inc.
2500 Rutland St.
Austin, TX 78766
(512) 836-1167

Central Scientific Co.
3300 Cenco Pkwy.
Franklin Park, IL 60131
(708) 451-0150
(800) 262-3626

Frey Scientific Co.
905 Hickory Lane
Manfield, OH 44905
(800) 225-3739

Midland Scientific, Inc.
1202 S. 11th St.
Omaha, NE 68108
(402) 346-8352

Nasco International, Inc.
901 Janesville Ave.
Fort Atkinson, WI 53538
(414) 563-2446
(800) 558-9595

Sargent-Welch Scientific Company
7300 N. Linden Ave.
P.O. Box 1026
Skokie, IL 60077
(800) 727-4368

Science & Things
30061 Plymouth Rd.
Livonia, MI 48150
(313) 422-8511

Science Explore Store
Science Museum of Minnesota
10th and Cedar
St. Paul, MN 55101
(612) 221-4705

WEST

A. Warren's Educational Supplies
7715 Garvey Ave.
Los Angeles, CA 91722
(800) 523-7767

Amico Scientific
1161 Cushman Ave.
San Diego, CA 92110
(619) 543-9200

Bryant Lab, Inc.
1101 Fifth St.
Berkeley, CA 94710
(510) 526-3141

Chem-Lab Supplies
1060-C Ortega Way
Placentia, CA 92670
(714) 630-7902

Cosco-Colorado Scientific Instrument
    & Supply Co.
900 Broadway
Denver, CO 80224
(303) 832-2811

Custom Lab Supply
801 98th Ave.
Oakland, CA 94603
(510) 633-1329

Educational Toys & Games
647 S. La Brea Ave.
Los Angeles, CA 90036
(213) 933-5691

Tri-Ess Sciences
1020 Chestnut St.
Burbank, CA 91506
(818) 848-7838

Universal Scientific of Arizona
320 S. El Dorado
Mesa, AZ 85202
(602) 966-2780

NORTHWEST

Carolina Biological Supply Co.
Gladstone, OR 97027
(503) 656-1641

Northwest Scientific, Inc.
421 N. 24th St.
Billings, MT 59103
(406) 252-3269

Scientific Supply & Equipment
926 Poplar Place, S.
Seattle, WA 98144
(206) 324-8550

APPENDIX C

STATE, REGIONAL, AND FOREIGN SCIENCE AND ENGINEERING FAIRS

There are currently over 400 state, regional, and foreign science and engineering fairs that are affiliated with the International Science and Engineering Fair. These fairs are held annually on various dates during the months of February through April. While these fairs play host to thousands of top science fair exhibits from students in grades 7 through 12, only students in grades 9 through 12 from these fairs are eligible to participate in the annual International Science and Engineering Fair, which is administered by Science Service, Inc.

Below is a complete listing of all affiliated fairs and their hosting cities. The names, addresses, and telephone numbers of fair administrators, as well as the specific dates of these fairs, have not been included because many change on a yearly basis. However, if you would like to obtain specific information about any of the listed fairs, contact: Science Service, Inc., 1719 N Street, N.W., Washington, D.C. 20036 (202) 785-2255.

UNITED STATES

Alabama

Auburn: East Alabama Science and Engineering Fair

Birmingham: Central Alabama Regional Science and Engineering Fair

Decatur: North Alabama Regional Science and Engineering Fair

Mobile: Mobile Regional Science Fair

Talladega: Northeast Alabama Regional Junior Academy Science Fair

Troy: Southeast Alabama Regional Science Fair

Tuscaloosa: West Alabama Regional Science Fair

Alaska

Anchorage: Alaska Science and Engineering Fair

Arizona

Prescott: Northern Arizona Regional Science and Engineering Fair

Sierra Vista: SSVEC's Youth Energy Science Fair

Tempe: Central Arizona Regional Science and Engineering Fair

Tucson: Southern Arizona Regional Science and Engineering Fair

Arkansas

Arkadelphia: South Central Arkansas Regional Science Fair

Batesville: North Central Arkansas Regional Science Fair

Camden: Southwest Arkansas Regional Science Fair

Conway: Arkansas State Science Fair

Fayetteville: Northwest Arkansas Regional Science and Engineering Fair

Hot Springs: West Central Regional Science Fair

Jonesboro: Northeast Arkansas Regional Science Fair

Little Rock: Central Arkansas Regional Science Fair

Monticello: Southeast Arkansas Regional Science Fair

California

Alhambra: Alhambra Science and Engineering Fair

Fresno: Central California Science and Engineering Fair

Los Angeles: CAMS Science Fair

Monterey: Monterey County Science and Engineering Fair

San Diego: Greater San Diego Science and Engineering Fair

San Francisco: San Francisco Bay Area Science Fair, Inc.

San Jose: Santa Clara Valley Science and Engineering Fair

West Hills: Chaminade Science Fair

Colorado

Alamosa: San Luis Valley Regional Science Fair

Colorado Springs: Pikes Peak Regional Science Fair

Denver: Denver Metropolitan Science Fair

Fort Collins: Colorado Science and Engineering Fair

Fort Morgan: Morgan-Washington Bi-County Science Fair

Grand Junction: Western Colorado Science Fair

Greeley: Longs Peak Science and Engineering Fair

Trinidad: Spanish Peaks Regional Science Fair

Connecticut

Danbury: Science Horizons, Inc., Science Fair and Symposium

Hartford: Connecticut State Science Fair

District of Columbia

Washington, D.C.: District of Columbia Citywide Science Fair

Florida

Avon Park: Heartland Regional Science and Engineering Fair

Bradenton: GTE-Manatee Regional Science and Engineering Fair

Bushnell: Sumter County Regional Science Fair

Crystal River: Citrus Regional Science and Engineering Fair

Daytona, South: Tomoka Region Science and Engineering Fair

Fort Lauderdale: East Broward County Science Fair

Fort Lauderdale: West Broward County Science Fair

Fort Myers: Thomas Alva Edison East Regional Science Fair

Fort Myers: Thomas Alva Edison Regional Science Fair

Fort Pierce: Treasure Coast Regional Science and Engineering Fair

Fort Walton Beach: Northeast Panhandle Regional Science and Engineering Fair

Fort Walton Beach: Southeast Panhandle Regional Science and Engineering Fair

Gainesville: Alachua Regional Science and Engineering Fair

Huason: GTE/PASCO Regional Science and Engineering Fair

Jacksonville: Northeast Florida Kiwanis Regional Science and Engineering Fair

Kissimmee: Osceola Regional Science Fair

Lake City: Suwannee Valley Regional Science and Engineering Fair

Lakeland: Polk County Regional Science and Engineering Fair

Marianna: Chipola Regional Science and Engineering Fair

Melbourne: South Brevard Science and Engineering Fair

Merritt Island: Brevard Intracoastal Regional Science and Engineering Fair

Miami: South Florida Science and Engineering Fairs I and II

Ocala: Big Springs Regional Science Fair

Orange Park: Clay Kiwanis Science Fair

Orlando: Orange County Regional Science and Engineering Fair

Palatka: Putnam Regional Science and Engineering Fair

Palmetto: State Science and Engineering Fair of Florida

Panama City: Florida Three Rivers Regional Science and Engineering Fair

Pensacola: West Panhandle Regional Science and Engineering Fair

Quincy: West Bend Regional Science and Engineering Fair

St. Augustine: River Region East Science Fair

St. Petersburg: Pinellas Regional Science and Engineering Fair

Sanford: Seminole County Regional Science and Engineering Fair

Sarasota: Sarasota Regional Science and Engineering Fair

Spring Hill: Hernando County Regional Science and Engineering Fairs—East and West

Stuart: Martin County Regional Science and Engineering Fair

Tallahassee: Capital Regional Science and Engineering Fair

Tampa: Hillsborough Regional Science Fair

Titusville: Brevard Mainlands Science and Engineering Fair

Vero Beach: Indian River Regional Science and Engineering Fair

West Palm Beach: Palm Beach County Science and Engineering Fairs— Region I and Region II

Georgia

Albany: Darton College Regional Science Fair

Athens: Georgia State Science and Engineering Fair

Atlanta: Atlanta Science and Mathematics Congress

Augusta: Central Savannah River Area Science and Engineering Fair

Brunswick: Coastal Georgia Regional Science and Engineering Fair

Calhoun: Calhoun Area Regional Science and Engineering Fair

Douglasville: Douglas County Area Regional Science and Engineering Fair

Dublin: Heart of Georgia RESA District Science Fair

Griffen: Griffen RESA Regional Science Fair

Milledgeville: Georgia College/ Oconee RESA Regional Science and Engineering Fair

Perry: Houston District Science and Engineering Fair

Savannah: First Congressional District Science and Engineering Fair

Hawaii

Honolulu: Hawaii Association of Independent Schools Science and Engineering Fair

Honolulu: Hawaii State Science and Engineering Fair

Kaneohe: Windward District Science and Engineering Fair

Pearl City: Central Oahu District Science and Engineering Fair

Waipahu: Leeward District Science and Engineering Fair

Idaho

St. Maries: St. Joe Valley Science and Engineering Fair

Illinois

Chicago: Chicago Public Schools Student Science Fairs—Region I and Region II

Edwardsville: Illinois Junior Academy of Science Region XII Science Fair

Peoria: Heart of Illinois Science and Engineering Fair

Springfield: Illinois Junior Academy of Science Region X Science Fair

Indiana

Angola: Northeastern Indiana Tri-State Regional Science Fair

Columbus: South Central Indiana Regional Science and Engineering Fair

Evansville: Tri-State Regional Science and Engineering Fair

Fort Wayne: Northeastern Indiana Regional Science and Engineering Fair

Hammond: Calumet Regional Science Fair

Hanover: Southeastern Indiana Regional Science Fair

Indianapolis: Central Indiana Regional Science and Engineering Fair

Indianapolis: Hoosier Science and Engineering Fair

Muncie: East Central Indiana Regional Science Fair

South Bend: Northern Indiana Regional Science and Engineering Fair

Terre Haute: West Central Indiana Regional Science and Engineering Fair

West Lafayette: Lafayette Regional Science and Engineering Fair

Westville: Northwestern Indiana Science and Engineering Fair

Iowa

Bettendorf: QCSEF and Symposium— Davenport Metro Area

Bettendorf: QCSEF and Symposium—
Greater Quad City Metro Area

Cedar Rapids: Eastern Iowa Science
and Engineering Fair

Des Moines: Iowa Hawkeye Science
Fair

Indianola: South Central Iowa Science
and Engineering Fair

Kansas

Wamego: Wamego Regional Science
and Engineering Fair

Kentucky

Bowling Green: Southern Kentucky
Regional Science Fair

Louisville: Louisville Regional Science
Fair

Morehead: Northeast Kentucky
Regional Science Fair

Louisiana

Baton Rouge: Louisiana Science and
Engineering Fair

Baton Rouge: Region VII—Capital
Science and Engineering Fair

Bossier City: Louisiana Region I
Science and Engineering Fair

Houma: Terrebonne Parish Science Fair

Lafayette: University of Southwestern
Louisiana Region VI Science Fair

Lake Charles: Louisiana Region V
Science and Engineering Fair

Lutcher: St. James Parish Science Fair

Monroe: Louisiana Region III Science
and Engineering Fair

Natchitoches: Louisiana Region IV
Science Fair

New Orleans: Greater New Orleans
Science and Engineering Fair

Ruston: Louisiana Region II Science
and Engineering Fair

Thibodaux: Louisiana Region X
Science and Engineering Fair

Maryland

Annapolis: Anne Arundel County
Science and Engineering Fair

Baltimore: Morgan State University
Science-Mathematics-Engineering
Fair

Frederick: Frederick County Science
and Engineering Fair

Frostburg: Western Maryland
Regional Science Expo

Gaithersburg: Montgomery Area
Science Fair

Hagerstown: Washington County
Science and Engineering Fair

Largo: Prince George's Area Science
Fair

Silver Spring: Blair, Einstein, Kennedy,
Springbrook Consortium Fair

Towson: Baltimore Science Fair

Massachusetts

Bridgewater: Massachusetts Region V
Science Fair

Cambridge: Massachusetts State
Science Fair

Somerville: Massachusetts Region IV
Science Fair

Michigan

Ann Arbor: Southeastern Michigan
Science Fair

Benton Harbor: Southwest Michigan
Science and Engineering Fair

Detroit: Science and Engineering Fairs
1, 2, 3, and 4 of Metropolitan
Detroit

Flint: Flint Area Science Fair

Saginaw: Saginaw County Science and Engineering Fair

Minnesota

Bemidji: Northern Minnesota Regional Science Fair

Crookston: Western Minnesota Regional Science Fair

Duluth: Northeast Minnesota Regional Science Fair

Mankato: South Central/North Minnesota Regional Science and Engineering Fair

Mankato: South Central/South Minnesota Regional Science and Engineering Fair

Mankato: Southwest/North Minnesota Regional Science and Engineering Fair

Mankato: Southwest/South Minnesota Regional Science and Engineering Fair

Minneapolis: St. Paul Science Fair

Minneapolis: Twin Cities Regional Science Fair

Minneapolis: Western Suburbs Science Fair

Rochester: Minnesota Academy of Science State Fair

Rochester: Rochester Public Schools Science Fair

St. Cloud: Central Minnesota Regional Science Fair and Research Paper Program

Winona: Southeast Minnesota Regional Science Fair

Mississippi

Biloxi: Mississippi Region VI Science and Engineering Fair

Booneville: Mississippi Region IV Science Fair

Greenville: Mississippi Region III Science and Engineering Fair

Hattiesburg: Mississippi Region I Science and Engineering Fair

Jackson: Mississippi Region II Science and Engineering Fair

Jackson: Mississippi State Science and Engineering Fair

Starkville: Mississippi Region V— North and Region V—South Science and Engineering Fairs

University: Mississippi Region VII Science and Engineering Fair

Missouri

Cape Girardeau: Southeast Missouri Regional Science Fair

Jefferson City: Lincoln University Regional Science Fair

Joplin: Missouri Southern Regional Science Fair

Kansas City: Greater Kansas City Science and Engineering Fair

Manchester: Greater St. Louis Science Fair

Rolla: South Central Missouri Regional Science and Engineering Fair

St. Joseph: Mid-America Regional Science and Engineering Fair

St. Peters: St. Charles-Lincoln County Regional Science and Engineering Fair

Springfield: Ozarks Science and Engineering Fair

Montana

Billings: Southeastern Montana Science and Engineering Fair

Butte: Southwestern Montana
Regional Science and Engineering
Fair

Great Falls: Montana Region II
Science and Engineering Fair

Havre: MSU-Northern Hi-Line
Regional Science and Engineering
Fair

Missoula: Montana Science Fair

Nebraska

Hildreth: Central Nebraska Science
and Engineering Fair

Nebraska City: Greater Nebraska
Science and Engineering Fair

Nevada

Elko: Elko County Science Fair

Las Vegas: Southern Nevada Science
Fair

Reno: Western Nevada Regional
Science Fair

New Jersey

Jersey City: Hudson County Science
Fair

Morristown: North Jersey Regional
Science Fair

Trenton: Mercer Science and
Engineering Fair

New Mexico

Albuquerque: Northwestern New
Mexico Regional Science and
Engineering Fair

Farmington: San Juan New Mexico
Regional Science and Engineering
Fair

Grants: Four Corners Regional
Science and Engineering Fair

Las Cruces: Southwestern New
Mexico Regional Science and
Engineering Fair

Las Vegas: Northeastern New Mexico
Regional Science and Engineering
Fair

Portales: Southeastern New Mexico
Regional Science and Engineering
Fair

Socorro: New Mexico Science and
Engineering Fair

New York

Poughkeepsie: Dutchess County
Science Fair

Purchase: Manhattanville Annual
Science Competition

Rochester: Central Western Section—
Science Teachers Association of
NY State Science Congress

Stony Brook: Long Island Science and
Engineering Fairs I, II, III, and IV

Syracuse: Greater Syracuse Scholastic
Science Fair

Troy: Greater Capitol Region Science
and Engineering Fair

Utica: Utica College Regional Science
Fair

North Carolina

Charlotte: Mecklenburg County
Science, Mathematics and
Engineering Fair

Charlotte: Southwest North Carolina
Regional Science, Mathematics
and Engineering Fair

Durham: NCSSM Science Fair

North Dakota

Devils Lake: North Central North
Dakota Regional Science and
Engineering Fair

Fargo: Southeast North Dakota Regional Science and Engineering Fair

Grand Forks: Northeast North Dakota Regional Science and Engineering Fair

Jamestown: Southeast Central North Dakota Science and Engineering Fair

Mandan: Southwest Central North Dakota Regional Science and Engineering Fair

Minot: North Dakota State Science and Engineering Fair

Minot: Northwest Central North Dakota Regional Science Fair

Mott: Southwest North Dakota Regional Science and Engineering Fair

Williston: Northwest North Dakota Regional Science Fair

Ohio

Archbold: Northwest Ohio Science and Engineering Fair

Athens: Southeastern Ohio Regional Science and Engineering Fair

Canton: Ohio Academy of Sciences District XIII Science Day

Cleveland: Northeastern Ohio Science and Engineering Fair

Columbus: Buckeye Regional Science Fair VI

Dayton: Dayton Science and Engineering Fair

Dayton: Montgomery County Science and Engineering Fair

Delaware: Buckeye Regional Science Fairs I, II, III, IV, and V

Delaware: Buckeye Science and Engineering Fair

Millersburg: Hugo H. and Mabel B. Young Science and Engineering Fair

Oklahoma

Ada: Oklahoma State Science and Engineering Fair

Alva: Northwestern Oklahoma State University Regional Science Fair

Ardmore: Southeastern Oklahoma Regional Science and Engineering Fair

Bartlesville: Bartlesville District Science Fair

Edmond: Central Oklahoma Regional Science Fair

Lawton: Cameron University Regional Science Fair

Miami: Northeastern Oklahoma A&M Science and Engineering Fair

Muskogee: Muskogee Regional Science and Engineering Fair

Oklahoma City: Oklahoma City Regional Science and Engineering Fair

Seminole: East Central Oklahoma Regional Science and Engineering Fair

Tulsa: Tulsa Regional Science and Engineering Fair

Wilburton: Eastern Oklahoma Regional Science and Engineering Fair

Oregon

Forest Grove: Northwest Science Exposition

Gold Beach: Southwestern Oregon Regional Science Exposition

Pennsylvania

Carlisle: Capital Area Science and Engineering Fair

Lancaster: Lancaster Science and Engineering Fair

Philadelphia: Ben Franklin Science Fair

Philadelphia: Benjamin Banneker Science Fair

Philadelphia: Delaware Valley Science Fair

Philadelphia: Marie Curie Science Fair

Pittsburgh: Pittsburgh Regional Science and Engineering Fair

Reading: Reading and Berks Science and Engineering Fair

York: York County Science and Engineering Fair

Rhode Island

Kingston: Rhode Island State Science Fair

South Carolina

Beaufort: Sea Island Regional Science Fair

Charleston: Low Country Science Fair

Columbia: Central South Carolina Region II Science Fair

Florence: Sand Hills Regional Science Fair

Greenville: Western South Carolina Region I Science Fair

Spartanburg: Piedmont South Carolina Region III Science Fair

South Dakota

Aberdeen: Northern South Dakota Science and Math Fair

Brookings: Eastern South Dakota Science and Engineering Fair

Mitchell: South Central South Dakota Science and Engineering Fair

Rapid City: High Plains Regional Science and Engineering Fair

Timber Lake: Northwest Area Schools Regional Science and Engineering Fair

Tennessee

Chattanooga: Chattanooga Regional Science and Engineering Fair

Cookeville: Cumberland Plateau Regional Science and Engineering Fair

Jackson: West Tennessee Regional Science Fair

Knoxville: Southern Appalachian Science and Engineering Fair

Memphis: Memphis-Shelby County Science and Engineering Fairs— North Region and South Region

Nashville: Middle Tennessee Science and Engineering Fair

Texas

Abilene: Spring Science Competition

Amarillo: High Plains Regional Science Fair

Austin: Texas State Science and Engineering Fair

College Station: Brazos Valley Regional Science and Engineering Fair

Corpus Christi: Coastal Bend Science and Engineering Competition

Dallas: Dallas Morning News–Toyota Regional Science and Engineering Fair

El Paso: Sun Country Science Fair

Fort Worth: Fort Worth Regional Science Fair

Harlingen: Rio Grande Valley Regional
Science Fair

Houston: Science and Engineering
Fair of Houston

Kilgore: East Texas Regional Science
Fair

Laredo: Laredo Independent School
District Science Fair

Laredo: United Independent School
District Regional Science Fair

Lubbock: South Plains Regional
Science and Engineering Fair

Odessa: Permian Basin Regional
Science Fair

San Angelo: District XI Texas Science
Fair

San Antonio: Alamo Regional Science
and Engineering Fairs I, II, and
III

Victoria: Texas Mid-Coast Regional
Science and Engineering Fair

Waco: Central Texas Science and
Engineering Fair

Wichita Falls: Red River Regional
Science and Engineering Fair

Utah

Blanding: Southeastern Utah Regional
Science and Engineering Fair

Bountiful: North Davis Area Science
and Engineering Fair

Brigham City: Box Elder Science and
Engineering Fair

Cedar City: Color Country Utah
Science and Engineering Fair

Cedar City: South Central Utah
Science and Engineering Fair

Cedar City: Southern Utah Science
and Engineering Fair

Cedar City: Southwest Utah Science
and Engineering Fair

Ogden: Ogden Area I Science and
Engineering Fair

Ogden: State Science and Engineering
Fair of Utah

Plain City: West Weber Area Science
and Engineering Fair

Pleasant View: North Weber Area
Science and Engineering Fair

Provo: Central Utah Science and
Engineering Fair

Roy: Roy Area Science and
Engineering Fair

Washington Terrace: Ogden South
Weber Science and Engineering
Fair

Virginia

Annandale: Virginia State Science and
Engineering Fair

Arlington: Northern Virginia Science
and Engineering Fair

Charlottesville: Piedmont Regional
Science Fair

Fairfax: Fairfax County Area Regional
Science and Engineering Fairs I,
II, III, and IV

Fairfax: Fairfax County Regional
Science and Engineering Fair—
Thomas Jefferson

Farmville: Southside Virginia Regional
Science Fair

Harrisonburg: Shenandoah Valley
Regional Science Fair

Hopewell: James River Regional
Science Fair

Lynchburg: Central Virginia Regional
Science Fair

Manassas: Prince William-Manassas
Regional Science Fair

Newport News: Tidewater Science
Fair

Roanoke: Western Virginia Regional
Science Fair

Sterling: Loudoun County Regional
Science Fair

Wise: Southwestern Virginia Regional
Science Fair

Wytheville: Blue Ridge Highlands
Regional Science Fair

Washington

Bremerton: Washington State Science
and Engineering Fair

Kennewick: Mid-Columbia Regional
Science and Engineering Fair

West Virginia

Elkins: Eastern Regional Science Fair

Keyser: West Virginia Eastern
Panhandle Regional Science Fair

Montgomery: Central West Virginia
Regional Science and Engineering
Fair

Princeton: Mercer County Science and
Engineering Fair

West Liberty: West Liberty State
College Regional Science and
Engineering Fair

West Liberty: West Virginia State
Science and Engineering Fair

Wisconsin

Milwaukee: National American Indian
Science and Engineering Fairs I,
II, and III

Milwaukee: Southeastern Wisconsin
Science and Engineering Fair

Wyoming

Cheyenne: Southeast Wyoming
Regional Science Fair

Laramie: Wyoming State Science Fair

OUTSIDE THE UNITED STATES

American Samoa

Pago Pago: American Samoa Science
Fair

Argentina

Concepción, Tucumán: Feria Provincial
de Ciencia y Tecnología Juvenil

Cordoba: Feria Nacional de Ciencia y
Tecnología Cordoba Argentina

Mendoza: IX Feria Internacional de
Ciencia y Tecnología Juvenil del
Cono Sur

Posadas, Misiones: Feria Provincial de
Ciencia y Tecnología

San Luis: National Science Fair of
Argentina

Tandil–Buenos Aires: Feria Local de
Ciencia y Tecnología

Tucumán: Instituto Tecnico Salesiano
Lorenzo Massa

Belgium

Brussels: Exposciences Des
Deunesses Scientifiques

Bolivia

Cochabamba: National Science Fair of
Bolivia

Brazil

Blumenau-SC: Blumenau Science Fair
of Brazil

Campo Grande: Paiaguas Clube de
Ciencias e Cultura

Novo Hamburgo: National Science
Fair of Brazil

Santa Cruz do Sul: Feria de Ciencias
da Escola Estadual Ernesto Alves
de Oliveira

Canada

Alberta: Canada-Wide Science Fair (CWSF)/Peace River Country Regional Science Fair

British Columbia: CWSF/Greater Vancouver Regional Science Fair

British Columbia: CWSF/Mainline-Caribou Regional Science Fair

British Columbia: CWSF/North Okanagan-Shuswap Regional Science Fair

British Columbia: CWSF/Vancouver Island Regional Science Fair

Manitoba: CWSF/Winnipeg Schools Regional Science Fair

Newfoundland: CWSF/Eastern Newfoundland Regional Science Fair

Nova Scotia: CWSF/Halifax-Dartmouth Regional Science Fair

Nova Scotia: CWSF/Kings County District Regional Science Fair

Northwest Territories: CWSF/N.S.S.S.S. Regional Science Fair

Hamilton, Ontario: Hamilton District Science and Engineering Fair

North Bay, Ontario: North Bay Regional Science Fair

Montreal, Quebec: Montreal Regional Science Fair

Ontario: CWSF/Kent Regional Science Fair

Ontario: CWSF/Kingston and District Regional Science Fair

Ontario: CWSF/Metro Toronto Regional Science Fair

Ontario: CWSF/Scarborough Regional Science Fair

Ontario: CWSF/Sudbury Regional Science Fair

Ontario: CWSF/Waterloo-Wellington Regional Science Fair

Ontario: CWSF/Windsor Regional Science Fair

Ottawa, Ontario: Canada-Wide Science Fair (CWSF)

St. Catharines, Ontario: Niagara Regional Science and Engineering Fair

Quebec: CWSF/Maurice Regional Science Fair

Quebec: CWSF/Montreal Regional Science Fair

Quebec: CWSF/Outaouais Regional Science Fair

Quebec: CWSF/Sagenay-Lac St. Jean Regional Science Fair

Saskatchewan: CWSF/Carlton Trail Regional Science Fair

Chile

La Cisterna-Santiago: Feria de Ciencia y Tecnología La Cisterna

Santiago: Feria Científica del Museo Nacional de Historia Natural

Santiago: Feria de Astronomía de Santiago

Santiago: National Science Fair of Chile

China

Shanghai: Shanghai Science Festival

Colombia

Medellín: Club Científico Omega

Zarzal, Valle del Cauca: Feria Distrital Juvenil de la Ciencia

Costa Rica

San Jose: Feria Nacional Juvenil Ciencia y Tecnología

209

European Union

Brussels, Belgium: European Union Contest for Young Scientists

Germany

Cologne: Young Europeans' Environmental Research Competition

Guam

Mangilao: Guam Island-Wide Science Fair

Hungary

Budapest: Innovation Contest for Young Scientists

Ireland

Dublin: Aer Lingus Young Scientists Exhibition

Jamaica

Kingston: Caribbean Science Fair

Japan

Tokyo: Japan Students Science Awards

Mexico

Monterrey, NL: Programa Emprendedor

New Zealand

Dunedin: ECNZ New Zealand Science Fair

Nigeria

Obalende, Lagos: Junior Engineers, Technicians and Scientists

Norway

Oslo: Young Scientists Contest

Paraguay

Asuncion: Feria Nacional de Ciencias y Tecnología

Peru

Jesús María-Lima: Ciencia y Tecnología Parte 2

Lima: Feria Escolar Nacional de Ciencia y Tecnología

Portugal

Porto: European Contest for Young Scientists

Puerto Rico

Aguadilla: Western Regional Mathematics Fair

Arecibo: Arecibo Regional Science Fair

Bayamon: Bayamon Regional Science Fairs I and II

Cavey: Private School Consortium Science and Engineering Fair

Gurabo: Caguas Educational Regional Science Fairs I, II, III, and IV

Humacao: Humacao Regional Science Fair

Ponce: Ponce Regional Science Fairs I, II, III, and IV

Rio Piedras: Eastern Regional Mathematics Fair

Rio Piedras: San Juan Archdiocesan Regions I, II, III, and IV Science Fairs

San German: InterAmerican University of Puerto Rico Regional Science Fair

San German: Mayaguez Educational Regional Science Fairs I, II, III, IV, V, and VI

San German: Puerto Rico State
Science Fairs I, II, III, and IV

San Juan: San Juan Educational Regional
Science Fairs I, II, III, and IV

Sweden

Stockholm: Utställningen Unga
Forskare

Switzerland

Winterthur: Schweizer Jugend Forscht

Taiwan

Taipei: Middle Taiwan Regional
Science Fair

Taipei: Republic of China (Taiwan)
National Science and Engineering
Fair

Taiwan: South Taiwan Regional
Science Fair

Ukraine

Kiev: Young Scientists Competition

United Kingdom

London: British Youth Science Fair

Uruguay

Mendoza: Feria Internacional de
Ciencia y Tecnología Juvenil

Montevideo: National Science Fair of
Uruguay

Punta del Este-Maldonado: Feria de
Ecología Aplicada

Venezuela

Caracas: Feria Científica y Tecnología
de Venezuela

APPENDIX D

ALTERNATIVE SCIENCE PROJECT COMPETITIONS

The emphasis of this book has been on the preparation of a science project for a traditional type of science fair. These fairs are usually state or regional competitions, affiliated with the International Science and Engineering Fair. However, some students preparing projects for traditional science fairs may also qualify to enter their work in other science competitions as well.

While there are numerous programs in existence, only the two oldest and better-known competitions are discussed here. However, if you would like to find out more information about other worthy science programs, scholarships, and competitions that you may be eligible for, consult the *National Advisory List of Contests and Activities* produced by the National Association of Secondary School Principals. Interested students and teachers may also wish to consult the reference book *Student Science Opportunities*, by Gail L. Grand, John Wiley & Sons, Inc., 1994. This worthwhile reference contains the names and addresses of many science opportunities available to students in grade school through college.

WESTINGHOUSE SCIENCE TALENT SEARCH

Considered by many to be the most prestigious of science project competitions (several of its alumni have gone on to become Nobel Laureates), the Westinghouse Science Talent Search has provided educational opportunities and scholarships to its finalists for over fifty years. It is conducted annually and is sponsored by the Westinghouse Electric Corporation and Science Service, Inc. The competition is open to high school seniors and is designed to recognize and develop ability in science, mathematics, and engineering.

Every year, the Westinghouse Science Talent Search selects the top 20 percent from the hundreds of fully qualified entrants as semifinalists. From this group, 40 finalists are chosen and awarded all-expense-paid trips to the Science Talent Institute in Washington, D.C., to compete for substantial college scholarships. A listing of the names of the finalists and semifinalists is distributed to all colleges and universities in the United States and is looked upon by many college recruiters as one of the highest recommendations a student can receive. As a result, many of these students have been successful in receiving scholarships.

To enter the Westinghouse Science Talent Search, graduating seniors must complete a research project and prepare a written report on it, which may not exceed 20 double-spaced typewritten pages. The student must also submit an official high school transcript, as well as SAT, PSAT, and any other available standardized test scores. In addition, the student must complete the official entry forms, which must be signed by a science advisor and school officials. Once complete, the student must mail his or her entry to Science Service by the end of November. In late January of the following year, the winners are announced.

In cooperation with the national competition, several states operate their own state Science Talent Search competitions. For more information on the Westinghouse Science Talent Search or on a particular state Science Talent Search, send a self-addressed, stamped envelope along with your inquiry to:

The Westinghouse Science Talent Search
c/o Science Service
1719 N Street, N.W.
Washington, D.C. 20036

THE NATIONAL JUNIOR SCIENCE AND HUMANITIES SYMPOSIUM

Since 1958, the National Junior Science and Humanities Symposium (JSHS) has recognized the accomplishments of high school students in science, mathematics, and engineering. It is funded by the U.S. Army Research Office and is administered by the Academy of Applied Science and Higher Education.

Currently, there are 46 regional symposia affiliated with the National JSHS, which are held annually at various college and university campuses mostly located in the United States. To qualify for the national competition, students must first be nominated by their school to participate in a regional symposium. If selected, the student submits a scientific research paper about the findings of his or her science project. Selected students then present their research papers at the regional symposium before a panel of judges. In addition, these students are given the opportunity to attend scientific lectures and tours and interact with scientists and engineers.

The top five contestants from each regional symposium are awarded all-expense-paid trips to attend the National JSHS. From this group, only one student is selected to compete for awards and scholarships with 45 other top regional students. Finally, the winners at the National JSHS advance to the London International Youth Science Forum which is held at London University.

In addition to the National JSHS, the Academy of Applied Science administers other worthwhile science programs for students. For more information about the National JSHS, its affiliated regional symposia, and other programs administered by the Academy of Applied Science, send a self-addressed, stamped envelope along with your inquiry to:

Doris Ellis Cousins
JSHS National Office
Academy of Applied Science
98 Washington Street
Concord, NH 03301

GLOSSARY

abstract   A brief summary of a science project (approx. 250 words) that explains the project's objective and procedure and provides generalized data and a workable solution to the problem addressed by the project.

backboard   A self-supporting bulletin board with a summary outline of a science project. The backboard contains the project title and topic progression, together with flowcharts, photographs, and other significant project descriptions. The backboard is usually organized according to the steps of the scientific method.

biological sciences category   A basic category encompassing several life sciences, including behavioral and social sciences, biochemistry, botany, ecology, genetics, medicine and health, microbiology, zoology, animal species studies, disease, etc.

clarity   A judging criterion that addresses whether a science project is presented in a concise fashion.

conclusion   The solution to a proposed issue and confirmation or rejection of a hypothesis.

control   A part of an experiment that provides a guideline for comparing an experimental group.

creative ability   A judging criterion that grades ingenuity and originality in an approach to a topic.

data   Recorded information that is organized for final analysis and observation.

dependent variable   The variable that is being measured.

display   The complete set-up of a science project. The display includes a backboard, a representation of the subject matter or experimental results, and a research report.

dramatic value   A judging criterion that addresses whether the project is presented in a way that attracts attention through the use of graphics and layout.

erroneous hypothesis   An incorrect or vague hypothesis that does not support the experimental results.

experiment   The part of the project in which the scientist tests to verify a law, explain a cause-and-effect relationship, measure efficiency, or observe an unexplained process.

experimental angle   The narrowed experimental option best suited to bringing about a desired or fitting solution to the issue.

frequency distribution   A mathematical summary of a set of data that shows the numerical frequency of each class of items.

histogram   A graph that represents a frequency distribution. The item classes are placed along the horizontal axis and the frequencies along the vertical axis. Rectangles are drawn, with the item class as the base and the frequency as the side.

hypothesis   An assumed or tentative guess as to the possible solution to a problem.

independent variable   The variable that is controlled or manipulated by the experimenter.

International Science and Engineering Fair (ISEF)   Since 1949, this science fair has been held for the top science fair projects from around the world. It is considered to be the "Super Bowl" of science fairs.

journal   A logbook used to record everything that the student has learned and completed with his or her project. Items to note include articles read, places visited, data results, etc.

line graph   A graph used to summarize information from a table. It has an x (horizontal) axis and a y (vertical) axis, where points are plotted at corresponding regions.

mean   The measurement of the central location of a group of data through the use of a mathematical average. The mean is denoted by the symbol $(\bar{x})$.

percentile   The position of one value from a set of data that expresses the percentage of the other data that lie below this value. The position of a particular percentile can be calculated by dividing the desired percentile by 100 and multiplying by the number of items in the ascending data set.

physical sciences category   A basic category including chemistry, math, earth and space science, engineering, physics, toxic waste, electronics, etc.

pie chart   A graph represented by a circle that is divided into segments. The circle represents the whole amount (100%), and each section represents a percentage of the whole.

primary sources   Those sources of information that consist of surveys, observations, and experiments done directly by the science student.

procedural plan   A uniform and systematic way of testing the subject matter. Procedural planning begins with correlating to determine variables and a uniform control group.

project display   The item(s) from a science project that can fully represent, exemplify, or explain research, experimentation, and conclusions.

project limitation guidelines   Guidelines established by the ISEF that explain how far a student may go in his or her research and experimentation.

purpose/objective   The goal of a project; the theme that requires greater development or understanding.

research   The process by which information about the issue at hand is collected to search for possible clues in the development of the purpose or objective.

research report   An in-depth discussion of an entire science project from start to finish, including a subject history, research experience, method applied, experimental angle used, data, conclusive remarks, glossary, photos, diagrams, etc.

science fair   An exhibition of selectively chosen science projects grouped into corresponding categories and marked for their quality. Science fairs occur on local, state, regional, and international levels. (The fairs discussed in this book refer to those affiliated with the International Science and Engineering Fair.)

science project   A project of a scientific nature that is done by students in grades 6–12 for a local, state, regional, or international science exhibition. The project employs a systematic approach in order to formulate a conclusion to a proposed scientific question. The science project is modeled after the scientific method.

scientific abstracts   Bound volumes of thousands of brief scientific discussions. Scientific abstracts are grouped into two classes: research and experimental. The abstracts discuss experimental reports and review scientific literature.

scientific method   An organized process used for developing a solution to a specific question or problem.

scientific thought   A judging criterion that addresses how a science project shows evidence of an applied scientific or engineering development through cause-and-effect, verification of laws, applied techniques for efficiency, or presentation of a new concept.

secondary sources   Sources of information written by outsiders and obtained through libraries, media, government agencies, or corporations.

skill   A judging criterion that grades a science project on how much scientific and engineering practice was employed. The level of experimentation, preparation, and treatment of the subject matter play an important role.

statistical method   A method used to further describe and summarize data results through the use of specialized numbers, graphs, and charts.

table   An orderly display of data, usually arranged in rows and columns.

tests and surveys   The techniques that endeavor to determine the relationship, if any, that exists between variables.

thoroughness   A judging criterion that addresses the variety and depth of the literature used, experimental investigation, and all the aspects of the project.

variable   Some characteristic of an object, environment, plant, animal, performance, or behavior that can take on two or more values.

INDEX